Chronic  **escents**

About the Authors

Ronald T. Brown, PhD, ABPP is Professor of Public Health, Psychology and Pediatrics and is Dean of the College of Health Professions at Temple University. Dr. Brown is a diplomate in Clinical Health Psychology of the American Board of Professional Psychology, and is a fellow of the American Psychological Association, the American Psychological Society, the Society of Behavioral Medicine, and the National Academy of Neuropsychology. Dr. Brown has been the recipient of numerous grant awards from the National Institutes of Health, the Centers for Disease Control and Prevention, the Department of Defense and the Office of Special Education and Rehabilitation Services. Dr. Brown currently is the Editor of the *Journal of Pediatric Psychology* and serves of the Behavioral Medicine and Intervention Outcomes of the Center for Scientific Review of the National Institutes of Health. He has published over 200 articles, chapters, and books related to childhood psychopathology and health psychology. He also has served on the editorial boards of 11 journals related to child and adolescent psychopathology. Dr. Brown also serves as a liaison to the American Academy of Pediatric subcommittee on the assessment and practice guidelines for attention-deficit/hyperactivity disorder. Dr. Brown also serves as Chair of the Board of Scientific Affairs of the American Psychological Association.

Brian P. Daly, PhD, is Assistant Professor in the Department of Public Health at Temple University. Dr. Daly is an Instructor in Health Psychology, Director of the Temple Children's Hospital pediatric psychology clinic, and practices clinically in the Department of Pediatrics, where he often consults and provides therapeutic interventions to children with chronic illnesses. Dr. Daly recently received a research award from the Pew Foundation to investigate prevention efforts with children at risk for behavioral problems. Dr. Daly's research interests include interventions for children and adolescents with chronic illnesses, sleep hygiene behaviors for children, school mental health services, and resiliency factors among urban children and adolescents of color.

Annette U. Rickel, PhD, is a Professor of Psychology at Cornell University Medical College in New York City and is in a clinical practice. She received her Doctorate from the University of Michigan, and is a fellow and past President of the American Psychological Association's Society for Community Research and Action, and was a fellow of the American Council on Education. Dr. Rickel was a Senior Congressional Science Fellow in the U.S. Senate from 1992–1994, and served on President Clinton's Task Force for National Health Care Reform. Dr. Rickel has received several research awards from institutions such as the National Institute of Mental Health, as well as the MacArthur and Kellogg Foundations. She has been a Consulting Editor for the American Journal of Community Psychology, the Journal of Community Psychology, and the Journal of Primary Prevention, and serves on the Board of Directors of many non-profit organizations. Dr. Rickel has authored or coauthored seven books, numerous research articles, and chapters that deal with early intervention programs for individuals at high risk for psychopathology.

Advances in Psychotherapy – Evidence-Based Practice

Danny Wedding; PhD, MPH, Prof., St. Louis, MO
(Series Editor)
Larry Beutler; PhD, Prof., Palo Alto, CA
Kenneth E. Freedland; PhD, Prof., St. Louis, MO
Linda C. Sobell; PhD, ABPP, Prof., Ft. Lauderdale, FL
David A. Wolfe; PhD, Prof., Toronto
(Associate Editors)

The basic objective of this new series is to provide therapists with practical, evidence-based treatment guidance for the most common disorders seen in clinical practice – and to do so in a "reader-friendly" manner. Each book in the series is both a compact "how-to-do" reference on a particular disorder for use by professional clinicians in their daily work, as well as an ideal educational resource for students and for practice-oriented continuing education.

The most important feature of the books is that they are practical and "reader-friendly:" All are structured similarly and all provide a compact and easy-to-follow guide to all aspects that are relevant in real-life practice. Tables, boxed clinical "pearls", marginal notes, and summary boxes assist orientation, while checklists provide tools for use in daily practice.

Chronic Illness in Children and Adolescents

Ronald T. Brown
College of Health Professions, Temple University, Philadelphia, PA

Brian P. Daly
College of Health Professions, Temple University, Philadelphia, PA

Annette U. Rickel
Cornell University Medical College, New York City, NY

HOGREFE

Library of Congress Cataloging in Publication

is available via the Library of Congress Marc Database under the
LC Control Number 2007928887

Library and Archives Canada Cataloguing in Publication

Brown, Ronald T.
    Chronic illness in children and adolescents / Ronald T. Brown, Brian
P. Daly, Annette U. Rickel.
Includes bibliographical references.
ISBN 978-0-88937-319-8
    1. Chronic diseases in children. 2. Chronic diseases in adolescence.
3. Chronically ill children. I. Daly, Brian P. II. Rickel, Annette U., 1941-
III. Title.
RJ380.B76 2007   618.92   C2007-903242-7

PUBLISHING OFFICES
USA: Hogrefe & Huber Publishers, 875 Massachusetts Avenue, 7th Floor,
                Cambridge, MA 02139
                Phone (866) 823-4726, Fax (617) 354-6875; E-mail info@hhpub.com
EUROPE: Hogrefe & Huber Publishers, Rohnsweg 25, 37085 Göttingen, Germany
                Phone +49 551 49609-0, Fax +49 551 49609-88, E-mail hh@hhpub.com

SALES & DISTRIBUTION
USA: Hogrefe & Huber Publishers, Customer Services Department,
                30 Amberwood Parkway, Ashland, OH 44805
                Phone (800) 228-3749, Fax (419) 281-6883, E-mail custserv@hhpub.com
EUROPE: Hogrefe & Huber Publishers, Rohnsweg 25, 37085 Göttingen, Germany
                Phone +49 551 49609-0, Fax +49 551 49609-88, E-mail hh@hhpub.com

OTHER OFFICES
CANADA: Hogrefe & Huber Publishers, 1543 Bayview Avenue, Toronto, Ontario M4G 3B5
SWITZERLAND: Hogrefe & Huber Publishers, Länggass-Strasse 76, CH-3000 Bern 9

Hogrefe & Huber Publishers
Incorporated and registered in the State of Washington, USA, and in Göttingen, Lower Saxony,
Germany

Printed and bound in the USA
ISBN 978-0-88937-319-8

Acknowledgments

To the children and adolescents with chronic illnesses and their families, we sincerely thank them for showing us the intensity of their strength and courage in the face of adversity. They all are amazing individuals and we are proud and fortunate to have collaboratively worked with them. The lessons learned from them continue to inspire us.

We are grateful for the support and love of our families. Dr. Daly particularly wishes to thank his wife, Kristin, whose encouragement was invaluable. Dr. Brown wishes to thank his wife, Kathy, and son, Ryan, who provide so much support for these endeavors. Dr. Rickel would like to acknowledge the continued enthusiasm of her son, Jay, in these accomplishments.

Table of Contents

Description

Management of chronic illness in children and adolescents often is a multi-faceted challenge that requires the attention and expertise of individuals from a variety of disciplines that include psychology, psychiatry, social work, and medicine. The aim of this book is to provide readers with a practical overview of the definitions, characteristics, theories and models, diagnostic and treatment indications, and relevant aspects and methods of evidence-based psychosocial treatments for chronic illness in children and adolescents. Although treatments and research for chronic conditions are reviewed in general, particular attention is directed at asthma, cancer, cystic fibrosis, diabetes mellitus, and sickle cell disease due to the high incidence of these chronic diseases among children and adolescents. Case vignettes and suggestions for further reading are provided for the interested reader.

1.1   Terminology

The *International Classification of Diseases,* 9th Revision, Clinical Modification (ICD-9-CM) names and codes for selected general medical conditions are found in Appendix G of the *Diagnostic and Statistical Manual of Mental Disorders,* Fourth Edition, Text Revision (DMS-IV-TR, American Psychiatric Association, 2000). The most recent ICD codes, ICD-10, were updated following publication of the DSM-IV-TR. Thus, because the DSM-IV-TR is the most recent version of the DSM, we describe conditions coded according to ICD-9-CM criteria. As part of the multiaxial assessment, these conditions should be listed on Axis III, General Medical Conditions. Below are a sample of the codes and names for common childhood and adolescent chronic illnesses listed in Appendix G of the DSM-IV-TR. It should be noted that this list represents only a sample of childhood chronic illnesses and is by no means exhaustive. Page limitations preclude a description of all chronic diseases.

Diseases of the Nervous System
- 345.10 Epilepsy, grand mal
- 345.40 Epilepsy, partial, with impairment of consciousness (temporal lobe)
- 345.50 Epilepsy, partial, without impairment of consciousness (Jacksonian)
- 345.00 Epilepsy, petit mal (absences)

Diseases of the Circulatory System
- 416.9 Chronic pulmonary heart disease

Diseases of the Respiratory System
- 493.20 Asthma, chronic obstructive
- 493.90 Asthma, unspecified
- 277.00 Cystic fibrosis

Neoplasms
- 208.10 Leukemia, chronic

Endocrine Diseases
- 250.00 Diabetes mellitus, type II/noninsulin-dependent
- 250.01 Diabetes mellitus, type I/insulin-dependent

Table 1
Pediatric Disorders from Major Pediatric Subspecialty Populations with Examples of Relevant Psychological Aspects

Subspecialty	Condition	Representative psychological aspects
Cardiology	Congenital heart defects	Impaired cognitive function secondary to hypoxia, parental guilt about responsibility for anomaly
	Acquired heart defects	Restriction of activity secondary to blood thinner used in valve replacement
	Hypertension	Cognitive/mood effects of antihypertensive medication
Endocrinology	Diabetes mellitus	Nonadherence with complex self-care regimen
Gastroenterology	Nonorganic recurrent abdominal pain	Reinforcement of child "sick" behavior, family dysfunction
	Iletis (Chron's disease)	Impaired self-esteem
Hematology	Sickle cell disease	Recurrent pain, cognitive changes
	Hemophilia	Chronic arthritic pain
Infectious disease	AIDS	Cognitive deterioration, depression
Neonatology	Brochopulmonary dysplasia	Feeding disorders, developmental delays
Nephrology	Renal failure	Treatment nonadherence, cognitive symptoms
	Cushing syndrome	Muscle weakness, body composition changes
Neurology	Seizures	Medication-induced changes in cognitive functioning
Oncology	Leukemia	Coping with adverse medical diagnostic and treatment procedures
	Solid tumors	Pain, treatment-related cognitive changes, death and dying issues

Nutritional Diseases
- 278.00 Obesity

Metabolic Diseases
- 275.1 Wilson's disease

Musculoskeletal System and Connective Tissue Diseases
- 714.00 Arthritis, rheumatoid
- 710.00 Systemic lupus erythematosus

Congenital Malformations, Deformations, and Chromosomal Abnormalities
- 741.90 Spina bifida

Infectious Diseases
- 042 HIV infection (symptomatic)

1.2   Definition

Chronic illness and physical disability (chronic health problems) generally refer to a disease state that has symptoms with a protracted course and involves

Chronic illness may affect a person's health status or psychological functioning

Table 2
Chronic Illness Terminology and Definitions

Term	Definition
Acute illness	A disease with an abrupt onset and usually a short course.
Adherence	The extent to which an individual's behavior agrees with advice given by health care providers.
Adaptation to illness	The psychological functioning and personal adjustment of children and adolescents who suffer from a chronic illness.
Chronic health problems	A health problem that lasts over three months, affects the child or adolescents normal activities, and requires lots of hospitalizations and/or home health care and/or extensive medical care.
Chronic illness	A disease state that has symptoms with a protracted course and involvement of one or more organ systems (e.g., brain, heart, lung, blood) and may impair health status or psychological functioning, and lasts three months or longer.
Coping	Changing thoughts and behaviors to manage distress and the problem underlying the distress in the context of a specific stressful encounter or situation.
Physical disability	Physical impairment that seriously limits one or more functional capacities.
Special health care needs	Children and adolescent who have or are at increased risk for a chronic physical, developmental, behavioral, or emotional condition and who also require health and related services of a type beyond that required by children generally.
Pain management	The process of attempting to alleviate or reduce pain.

one or more organ systems (e.g., brain, heart, lung, blood) and may impair health status or psychological functioning (Brown, 2006). Conditions are defined as chronic when they persist for more than three months within one year, affect the child's typical functioning and normal activities, and require ongoing care from one or more health care providers (Wallander, Thompson, & Alriksson-Smith, 2003). Some examples of chronic conditions include (but are not limited to): severe asthma, birth defects, type I and type II diabetes mellitus, congenital heart disease, depression, developmental disabilities, juvenile rheumatoid arthritis, cerebral palsy, muscular dystrophy, sickle cell disease, hemophilia, cystic fibrosis, cancer, head injuries, epilepsy, spina bifida, and HIV/AIDS.

Acute illness episodes last less than three months

An acute illness differs from a chronic illness in that it comes about suddenly and often has an identifiable cause. Generally, acute illnesses may be readily treated and the patient often experiences a return to normal health. These acute episodes tend to last less than three months. Some examples of acute illness include appendicitis, ear infection, and pneumonia. In contrast, a chronic illness often begins gradually, may have an uncertain etiology, and has multiple risk factors. Although chronic illnesses may be managed medically, they are rarely able to be completely cured and often persist for extended periods of time and even sometimes for life (Wallander et al., 2003). For these reasons, some children and adolescents with a chronic illness and their families may often experience high levels of stress and consequently require substantial amounts of time, energy, and personal resources in order to cope with the stressors and demands associated with their illness (Stein & Jessop, 1989).

1.3   Epidemiology

There is still debate about whether to use a categorical or noncategorical approach when classifying a chronic illness

Assessing the epidemiology of chronic illness in children and adolescents is difficult because of a multitude of factors, with the most significant being the lack of a consensus definition used to determine the specific illnesses to be included under the category of chronic illness (Seiffge-Krenke, 2001). Included within the domain of chronic illness are children with chronic physical illnesses, various forms of disability, and special health care needs. Attempts to reach a consensus definition have been further complicated by the fact that each chronic physical condition has a distinct biological process and pathophysiology, and the fact that specific treatments are generally designed for specific conditions (Brown, 2006). In addition, there is considerable debate in the pediatric psychology literature about whether to apply a categorical (disease specific) or noncategorical approach when classifying a chronic illness.

The categorical approach posits that each chronic illness or condition is associated with a unique set of psychosocial challenges (Reiter-Purtill & Noll, 2003). The strengths of this approach include the specificity of findings and ease of communication. A clear limitation of the categorical approach is that one third to one fifth of children with chronic illnesses have more than one chronic condition. The noncategorical approach recognizes that irrespective of illness type or condition, young people living with a chronic illness experience common stressors and face many similar life concerns that may result in psychological and social difficulties (Rolland, 1987; Stein & Jessop, 1982). The noncategorical approach allows for the study of specific topics (e.g., stress and coping) across illness groups, and it also allows for greater generalization with regard to all chronic conditions.

Although the majority of early research on pediatric chronic illness used categorical models, more recent studies have favored the noncategorical approach in understanding the psychosocial functioning of children and adolescents (e.g., Garstein, Short, Vannatta, & Noll, 1999; Wallander & Varni, 1998). Studies that use the noncategorical approach have demonstrated that there are few specific differences between disease groups (Meijer, Sinnema, Bijstra, Mellenbergh, & Wolters, 2000a; Nassau & Drotar, 1995), with some differences in psychological functioning being associated with functional impairments, restriction of activities (Meijer, Sinnema, Bijstra, Mellenbergh, & Wolters, 2000b), or central nervous system (CNS) dysfunction (Noll, Ris, Davies, Bukowski, & Koontz, 1992).

There also is a lack of quality data specifically focusing on chronic illness in children and adolescents, and there continues to be significant variance in methodology used to investigate the psychological functioning of various illnesses across these pediatric age ranges (Suris, 1995; Westbrook & Stein, 1994). Differences in methodology include the method of data collection (self-report vs. interview), and selection of the study participants (clinical vs. population-based samples), that may result in discrepancies in epidemiological data with regard to the psychiatric functioning of children and adolescents who suffer from chronic disease. Finally, the majority of childhood chronic conditions are rare, with the exception of asthma, psychiatric disturbances (e.g., attention-deficit/hyperactivity disorder and depression), and developmental delay. As a result of the scant literature in these areas, there is often less familiarity and experience with these conditions among mental health professionals (Perrin & MacLean, 1988).

1.3.1 Incidence and Prevalence

Narrowly defined definitions of chronic illness result in an approximate prevalence rate of 7% among adolescents (Newacheck & Stoddard, 1994). In contrast, broader definitions of chronic illness that include conditions such as mild asthma or correctable vision may raise the prevalence rate for adolescents as high as 15% (Suris, Michaud, & Viner, 2004). Recent estimates that include school-age children and adolescents suggest that between 20% and 30% of children in the U.S. (approximately 12–18 million) have a significant ongoing health care need related to a chronic health condition (Newacheck et al., 1998). However, prevalence estimates may further be defined by the functional impairment associated with the illness or the influence of the illness on the adolescent's daily functioning. Approximately two thirds of children experience mild conditions (not limited in activities); 29% experience moderate severity (limiting of some activity); and 5% experience severe conditions (significant bother and limitation of activity) (Newacheck & Taylor, 1992).

Recent evidence suggests that the prevalence rate of children and adolescents with chronic disability may be lower in the United States when compared

Table 3
Prevalence Rates of Chronic Illnesses in Childhood and Adolescence

| Illness | Prevalence Rate (%) | |
	Gortmaker et al. (1990) (0–15 Years)	Newacheck & Taylor (1992) (10–17 Years)
Asthma	2.93	4.68
Cancers and tumors	0.06	—
Cystic fibrosis	0.03	—
Diabetes mellitus	0.10	0.15
Sickle cell anemia	0.09	—

The lowest rate of chronic disability is in the United States when compared to other industrialized countries

The general prevalence of chronic illness among children and adolescents is rising

There are higher rates of chronic illness among individuals of lower socioeconomic status

to other industrialized countries. Merrick and Carmeli (2003) reviewed recent studies that examined the prevalence rates of chronic disability in Scandinavia, Israel, and the United States. The lowest rate of disability (5.8%) was found in the United States, and the highest prevalence in Finland (9.8%).

More importantly, the general prevalence of chronic illness among children and adolescents is rising, such that the percentage of children with severe long-term disease has more than doubled over the past two decades (Brown, 2006). Earlier detection of chronic illness, advances in biomedical science and medical care, and significant improvements in disease management that reduce mortality may partly account for the rising prevalence rates (Stein & Silver, 1999). Therefore, many children and adolescents who previously would have succumbed to their illness in previous years are now living well into their adult years.

Global epidemiological surveys have indicated higher rates of chronic illness among males, rural residents, individuals of lower socioeconomic status (SES), individuals residing in impoverished areas within countries, and among adolescents living in less educated families (Newacheck, 1994; Suris, 1995; van Dyck, Kogan, McPherson, Weissman, & Newacheck, 2004; Weiland, Pless, & Roghmann, 1992). In addition, variability has been noted with respect to specific conditions as they pertain to various social class and ethnic groups. For example, asthma is most prevalent in children from low-income and minority groups (Miller, 2000). Moreover, African-American children are roughly three times more likely to be hospitalized for asthma than are their Caucasian peers – 55.9 per 10,000 African-American children versus 16.2 per 10,000 Caucasian children ranging in age from birth to 17 years in 2001 (National Healthcare Quality/Disparities Reports [NHQDR], 2004) Additional examples include cystic fibrosis, which primarily affects Caucasians, and sickle-cell disease, which primarily affects African-Americans (Thompson & Gustafson, 1996).

1.4   Course and Prognosis

With the improved prognosis of many pediatric diseases, it is estimated that up to 98% of children diagnosed with a chronic illness now live to be at least 20 years old (van Dyck et al., 2004), depending on the condition. Thus, some diseases that previously significantly limited life expectancy are now considered chronic illnesses, whereas some illnesses and diseases are now cured.

For those children whose condition remains constant, most will not be able to lead normal lives without specialized care or management (Stein & Jessop, 1989). Children with chronic illnesses are also more likely than healthy children to have frequent physician and hospital visits (Newacheck et al., 1998). Additionally, among noninjury causes, chronic illness now accounts for the majority of children's hospital days and deaths (Wise, 2004). Those children whose illness is sufficient to limit most normative activities account for nearly one quarter of all school absences, one fifth of physician visits, and one third of days hospitalized (Newacheck & Taylor, 1992). It is estimated that approximately one half of young people with significant chronic illness are severely compromised in educational activities (Sexson & Madan-Swain, 1993). Despite these concerns, proper care and management may still help these children achieve near-typical functioning in their daily lives.

Many factors may affect the course of a chronic illness, including heredity, lifestyle (stress), behavioral factors (e.g., diet, exercise, treatment nonadherence, substance abuse, neurological impairments), and even environmental factors. It is noteworthy that chronic illnesses beginning in childhood present a special challenge to the quality of life (QOL) and life expectancy of both children and adolescents. Thus, when thinking about chronic illness, it is important to be familiar with the psychosocial implications of chronic illness. The onset of a chronic illness may be either acute or gradual with the course being progressive, constant, or relapsing. Outcomes for chronic illness often include shortened lifespan or death. Given that various chronic illnesses have different onsets, courses, and outcomes, we present a summary of the incidence, onsets, course, and prognosis of some of the more frequent chronic child and adolescent conditions.

> **Factors that affect chronic illness include heredity, lifestyle, behavioral factors, and environmental factors**

1.4.1   Asthma

Asthma is characterized as a chronic inflammatory disorder of the airways that involves intermittent and variable periods of airway obstruction (National Institutes of Health [NIH], 1997). Bronchial asthma affects over six million children and adolescents under the age of 18, and it is the leading cause of chronic illness among children and adolescents in the United States (Centers for Disease Control and Prevention [CDC], 1996). Findings from the 2001 National Health Interview Survey (NHIS; CDC, 2003) indicate that 13% of children under age 18 have been diagnosed with asthma, and 6% have had an asthma attack in the past twelve months.

Asthma causes more school absences each year (about 10 million) than any other chronic disease and is the third most common reason children under the age of 15 years are hospitalized (Taylor & Newacheck, 1992). The estimated annual cost of treating asthma in children in the United States during 1999 was $3.2 billion, resulting in a significant economic burden to patients, their families, health care providers, and society. What is most troubling about this disease is that studies have demonstrated an increasing prevalence of asthma

> **Asthma is the leading cause of chronic illness among children and adolescents in the United States**

morbidity and mortality, despite the availability of innovative and effective therapies to manage this disease (Weiss, 1996). Further, pediatric asthma disproportionately affects ethnic minority youth, urban communities, and low-income populations (Crain, Kercsmar, Weiss, Mitchell, & Lynn, 1998; Evans, 1992). For example, prevalence rates in diagnosed asthma are higher for African-Americans (15.7%) than for Caucasians (12.2%), but lowest for Hispanics (11.2%). Finally, rates are higher for poor children (15.8%) than nonpoor children (12%) (Akinbami, LaFleur, & Schoendorf, 2002).

The course of asthma varies considerably across patients (Young, 1994). The majority of children experience episodic illness, with extended symptom-free periods (intermittent asthma). In contrast, some children experience more con-tinuous episodes and, in the absence of continuous therapy, do not have extended symptom-free periods (chronic asthma) (Thompson & Gustafson, 1996). Children who suffer from seasonal allergies may experience virtually daily symptoms during an inhalant allergy season (seasonal asthma). Finally, severe asthma leading to death has been noted in a very small percentage of school children, with hypoxia being the primary cause of death (Evans et al., 1987). Frequently, this outcome has been associated with poor asthma management.

Studies that have examined the natural history of asthma from childhood to adulthood have found that it may be self-limited and remit over time, or it may persist and worsen in adulthood (Limb et al., 2005), indicating significant individual variability over the course of time. In general, factors that predict the persistence of asthma into adulthood include an early age at onset, severity of childhood asthma, and the degree of atopy (a response to common environ-mental allergens) (Zeiger, Dawson, & Weiss, 1999). Overall, for children with asthma, one third will experience spontaneous symptom remission by puberty (Seiffge-Krenke, 2001), with one half or more outgrowing the condition by adulthood. With proper treatment and a team approach to managing asthma, including family participation, most affected children can be expected to live a normal life. However, the prognosis is more guarded for children and adoles-cents who do not adhere to their prescribed treatment regimen.

1.4.2   Cancer

Cancer is the leading cause of death by disease for children under the age of 15 years

Every year, approximately 12,500 children and adolescents are diagnosed with cancer in the United States. In contrast to adults, cancer in children and adolescents is still considered rare, as only 1% of all cancers occur in the pediatric age group (Seiffge-Krenke, 2001). Nonetheless, cancer is the leading cause of death by disease for children under the age of 15 years (Mulhern & Butler, 2004). The most prevalent childhood cancers are acute lymphoblastic leukemia (ALL) and malignant brain tumors.

The course of cancer in children depends on a multitude of factors, includ-ing type of cancer, age at diagnosis, and initial symptomatology. On the basis of these factors, among others, children are classified into low-, medium-, or high-risk categories, which determine the intensity of their treatments (Cecalupo, 1994). Fortunately, due to the recent significant advances in vari-ous chemotherapies, there has been marked improvement in the survival rate among children and adolescent with cancer. For example, recent data indicate a cure rate exceeding 80% for children diagnosed with ALL (Mulhern & Butler, 2004).

1.4.3   Cystic Fibrosis

Cystic fibrosis (CF) is a genetically inherited disease that affects sodium channels in the body and causes respiratory and digestive problems. CF affects the mucus and sweat glands of the body and is caused by a defective gene (Lewiston, 1985). Thick mucus is formed in the breathing passages of the lungs and this predisposes the person to chronic lung infections (Levitan, 1989). Recent data from the 2003 Cystic Fibrosis Foundation Registry indicate that approximately 1 in 3,500 children in the United States each year is born with CF. Overall, approximately 30,000 children and adults in the United States, primarily Caucasian, are affected by CF (Cystic Fibrosis Foundation, 2003).

Cystic fibrosis is a genetically inherited disease

More than 80% of patients are diagnosed with CF by age three (Cystic Fibrosis Foundation, 2003). The course varies greatly from patient to patient, and is largely determined by the degree of pulmonary involvement. Among children, CF represents the most common lethal genetic disorder among Caucasians in the United States (Wagener, Sontag, Sagel, & Accurso, 2004). With recent advances in detection and management, the median age of survival for a person with CF is in the early to mid 30s (Cystic Fibrosis Foundation, 2003). This represents a dramatic increase in survival over the last three decades. Deterioration is inevitable in patients with CF, leading to debilitation and eventual death, usually from a combination of lung complications and cor pulmonale (an alteration in the structure and function of the right ventricle caused by a primary disorder of the respiratory system).

1.4.4   Diabetes Mellitus

Diabetes mellitus (DM) is a chronic metabolic disorder caused by an absolute or relative deficiency of insulin. Approximately 1.6 million children have diabetes (Centers for Disease Control and Prevention, 2000), making it the most common metabolic disease of childhood and adolescence. Type I DM, formerly referred to as insulin-dependent diabetes mellitus, juvenile diabetes, or childhood diabetes, occurs in approximately 1 in 500–600 children (Wysocki, Greco, & Buckloh, 2003) and usually begins during childhood or adolescence. Type I DM results from the absence, destruction, or loss of beta cells of the islets of Langerhans in the pancreas that causes an absolute deficiency of insulin. Type II DM, formerly known as adult-onset diabetes because it was uncommon in children, has been reported among U.S. children and adolescents with increasing frequency, and presently accounts for 10% to 20% of new cases of diabetes in youth. Type II DM begins when the body develops a resistance to insulin and no longer uses insulin properly. As the child's or adolescent's need for insulin rises, the pancreas gradually loses its ability to produce sufficient amounts of insulin to regulate blood sugar.

Type I diabetes mellitus usually begins during childhood or adolescence

Results from the National Health Interview Study revealed a prevalence of DM of 150 cases in 100,000 children and adolescents who were between the ages of 10 and 17 years (Newacheck & Taylor, 1992). A lower prevalence rate of 60 per 100,000 was reported for younger children in this study. Caucasians have the highest reported incidence of type I DM. In contrast, the incidence of type II DM is disproportionately higher among African-American, Native-American, and Hispanic populations (Wysocki et al., 2003).

Type I DM has little immediate morbidity, with the exception of severe diabetes ketoacidosis or hypoglycemia. Diabetic ketoacidosis (DKA) is a life-threatening condition that develops when cells in the body are unable to get the sugar (glucose) they need for energy. It can occur in children and adults who have little or no insulin in their bodies (mostly people with type I DM) when their blood sugar levels are high. Ketoacidosis can be caused by not taking enough insulin, having a severe infection or other illness, becoming severely dehydrated, or some combination of these factors. Hypoglycemia, also called low blood sugar, occurs when the blood glucose (blood sugar) level drops too low to provide enough energy for the body's activities. Hypoglycemia may be caused by certain medications, alcohol, certain cancers, critical illnesses such as kidney, liver, or heart failure, hormonal deficiencies, and disorders that result in the body producing too much insulin. Both forms of diabetes may be controlled by diet, exercise, oral medications, and insulin injections. Both type I and type II DM raise a person's risk for heart disease, stroke, and damage to the kidneys and eyes. In addition, uncontrolled diabetes is the leading cause of blindness, kidney disease, and amputations of arms and legs.

1.4.5   Sickle Cell Disease

Children with sickle cell disease often suffer from pain crises

Sickle cell disease (SCD) represents a spectrum of inherited disorders of red blood cells that is characterized by pain episodes, anemia (shortage of red blood cells), serious infections, and damage to vital organs (Lemanek, Ranalli, Green, Biega, & Lupia, 2003). These symptoms are caused by abnormal hemo-globin. In the Unites States, SCD affects approximately 72,000 people, most of whose ancestors come from Africa, although it is also present in people of Mediterranean, Indian, and Middle Eastern heritage (Charache, Lubin, & Reid, 1989). SCD is much more common in certain ethnic groups, occurring in approximately 1 in every 500 African Americans births and in 1 in every 1,000 to 1,400 Hispanic American births (National Heart, Lung, and Blood Institute [NHLBI], 1996).

Sickle cell disease is characteristically varied in its course between and within affected individuals (Ballas, 1991), but may include exacerbations that can become life threatening at any time. The frequency, severity, and nature of specific complications in any given individual are all important factors in predicting prognosis. For example, although infection is the leading cause of death in affected children aged 1–3 years, strokes and trauma are the leading causes of death in patients aged 10–20 years (Davis, Schoendorf, Gergen, & Moore, 1997). Recent estimates document that 80% of children with sickle cell disease will live into the third decade of life (Quinn, Rogers, & Buchanan, 2004). Early detection and comprehensive medical care have greatly improved the quality of life for people with sickle cell disease such that many are in fairly good health most of the time.

1.5   Differential Diagnosis

Recent research has demonstrated that there are several commonalities in psychosocial functioning across chronic conditions and disabilities (Brown, 2006). For example, the literature on adjustment and adaptation among specific disease categories has revealed few differences (Wallander et al., 2003). In addition, families of children with chronic disease and illness face remarkably similar problems. Thus, many experts have considered chronic illness and associated psychiatric symptoms as a general issue rather than a disease specific issue. For this reason, the psychosocial study of children and adolescents with a chronic illness has moved decidedly toward a noncategorical approach. Noncategorical approaches focus on the person or child involved rather than on a specific condition or pathological diagnosis. Within the framework of a noncategorical approach, children and adolescents with a chronic illness are believed to have problems with adjustment because they are exposed to nonspecific disease factors such as negative life-events and related stressors. Thus, adjustment is posited to be predicted by specific stressors other than by the disease itself.

Given the commonalities in psychosocial functioning across chronic conditions and disabilities, Wallander and colleagues (2003) recommend the examination of specific disease dimensions. These dimensions include psychosocial effects associated with the nature of onset and course of the disease, life threat potential, intrusiveness, or plan of treatment, visibility and social stigma, stability versus crisis, and secondary and functional cognitive disability. Additional dimensions include whether the illness is congenital or acquired, limitations of age appropriate activity and other functional limitations, mobility, physiological functioning, emotional/social impairment, sensory functioning, and communication impairment (Perrin, Newacheck, & Pless, 1993).

In psychology, differential diagnosis may be defined as the process of distinguishing one mental disorder from other disorders that share similar symptoms. In medicine, differential diagnosis may be defined as the process of weighing the probability of one disease versus that of other diseases possibly accounting for a patient's illness. Clearly, there are some commonalities between the definitions used in psychology and medicine; Nonetheless, the process by which the differential diagnosis is made for psychological and medical disorders (e.g., type I diabetes) also entails different procedures. For example, psychological diagnoses are typically based on, among other factors, clinical interviews, thorough history, rating scales and checklists, and symptom criteria from the DSM-IV-TR. In contrast, medical diagnoses, including chronic illnesses, are often based on, among other factors, a clinical interview, thorough history, physical examination, and laboratory tests (e.g., blood count, basic chemistries, and urinalysis).

Differential diagnosis in children and adolescents with a chronic illness may be particularly tricky as many psychiatric diseases are characterized by physical symptoms, and the astute pediatric psychologist needs to be aware of this diagnostic challenge. Frequently, physical symptoms that are determined to be manifestations of a depressive disorder may actually be the result of the medical disease itself (Shemesh et al., 2005). For example, a child receiving treatment for cancer may also appear to be depressed as a result of complaints of lethargy and poor concentration; However, these symptoms are also associated with the side effects of chemotherapy. Indeed, given the significant overlap between medical and psychiatric symptoms, some researchers have proposed that the behavioral and emotional problems of chronically ill children should be viewed as variations within the range of "normal" responses to abnormal situations and not as frank psychopathology (see Eiser, 1990). Therefore, accurately determining the incidence and etiology of psychiatric comorbid disorders among children and adolescents with a chronic illness is especially challenging because of the overlap between many medical and psychiatric symptoms.

Differential diagnosis for children and adolescents with a chronic illness is complex due to the overlap between many medical and psychiatric symptoms

There are several psychological classifications or syndromes that may resemble the physical symptoms often associated with chronic illness. For example, somatoform disorders present in children and adolescents consist of the persistent experience and complaints of somatic distress that cannot be fully explained by a medical diagnosis. These disorders include somatization disorder, conversion disorder, pain disorder, hypochondriasis, and body dysmorphic disorder. They are often diagnosed when appropriate medical examination reveals no organic basis for the complaint or when symptoms related to an identified organic disorder are much more severe than would typically be expected from an organic disorder (Campo & Fritsch, 1994). Practitioners making a differential diagnosis between somatic disorders and physical disorders need to be especially careful given that the presence of physical symptoms or painful complaints of unknown etiology is a fairly common occurrence in pediatric populations (Campo & Fritsch, 1994; Garralda, 1996). The astute practitioner should always consider the possibility that there is an organic etiology for a child's physical complaint. Common forms of somatization found in pediatric populations include headaches, recurrent abdominal pains, limb pains, fatigue, dizziness, and chest pain (Egger, Costello, Erkanli, & Angold, 1999). Therapeutic interventions for children with somatoform disorders include education, changes in reinforcement, and development of coping skills (Haugaard, 2004).

An adjustment disorder is a type of mental disorder resulting from maladaptive, or unhealthy responses to stressful or psychologically distressing life events, including the diagnosis of a chronic illness. In order to be classified as an adjustment disorder, the behavioral and emotional symptoms commonly associated with this disorder must be demonstrated to be a response to an identifiable stressor that has occurred within the past three months. The stressor may be acute (e.g., pneumonia) or chronic (e.g., sickle cell disease). Therefore, in the case of children with chronic illness, the diagnosis of adjustment disorder is typically made *after* the diagnosis of the medical condition.

1.6   Comorbidities

Although most children adapt successfully to their chronic condition, the limited literature on psychiatric disorders or adjustment disorders among children and adolescents with chronic illnesses suggests that, in general, children with chronic medical conditions are at heightened risk for secondary behavioral and emotional difficulties relative to their healthy peers (Thompson & Gustafson, 1996). Lavigne and Faier-Routman (1992) conducted a meta-analysis to examine psychological adjustment among children with chronic illness. Results revealed higher levels of total adjustment difficulties, internalizing (e.g., anxiety, depression), externalizing problems (e.g., attention-deficit/hyperactivity disorder [ADHD], conduct disorder, acting-out behaviors), and lower levels of self-esteem in children with chronic illnesses when compared to nondisease comparison controls.

One recent study compared adolescents with various chronic illnesses with a healthy group of adolescents (Key, Brown, Marsh, Spratt, & Recknor, 2001), and found that a higher percentage of adolescents with a chronic illness reported symptoms of moderate to severe depression. Barlow and Ellard (2006) conducted a recent meta-analysis of studies that assessed the psychosocial well-being of children with a chronic disease. A total of 391 studies were reviewed; of these only 10 met criteria for inclusion in the meta-analysis, with three reviews focusing on chronic disease in general. Children with chronic illness were at slightly elevated risk for psychosocial distress compared to their healthy peers, although only a minority experienced clinical symptomatology. Finally, it is noteworthy that a minority of chronically ill children exhibit significant maladjustment (Eiser, 1990). Taken together, these findings suggest that children with a chronic illness cannot be treated as a homogenous group. Rather, some children may demonstrate resiliency in the face of chronic illness while others may experience significant psychosocial problems. Finally, that Barlow and Ellard (2006) were only able to evaluate 10 studies for their meta-analysis highlights the importance of mounting additional well-controlled, rigorously designed studies that evaluate the psychosocial well-being of children and adolescents with chronic illness.

Risk for emotional difficulties may be associated with the specific condition or degree of functional impairment associated with the illness. For example, Bennett (1994) conducted a review of 60 studies of children ranging in age from 4 to 18 years who were identified as having various chronic medical problems. Bennett concluded that among children with certain specific disorders (e.g., asthma, recurrent abdominal pain, and sickle cell anemia), risk was greater for depressive symptomatology than for children with other disorders (e.g., cancer, cystic fibrosis, and diabetes mellitus). Findings from the study by Key and colleagues (2001) demonstrate that the frequency of self-reported depressive symptomatology was highest in those adolescents with sickle cell disease as compared to other chronic illnesses. In addition, children with a chronic illness other than asthma or cancer may be at increased risk for a mood disorder (e.g., dysthymia, hypomania, major depression, mania), but there is no increased risk for anxiety disorders (Ortega, Huertas, Canino, Ramirez, & Rubio-Stipec, 2002).

The astute practitioner needs to determine whether the emotional and behavioral problems are actually comborbid with the medical illness. In some cases, emotional and/or behavioral difficulties are actually present *before* the diagnosis of a chronic illness, yet may affect the child or adolescent's adaptation to the illness and adherence to the recommended treatment regimen (Anderson, Brown, & Williams, 1999). For example, an adolescent with ADHD would be expected to have difficulty managing tasks associated with type I diabetes, including resisting foods with sugar, measuring insulin, etc.

Brief descriptions of common chronic illnesses and possible associated comorbid psychiatric conditions are presented in the following sections.

Children with chronic medical conditions, in general, are at increased risk for secondary behavioral and emotional difficulties relative to their healthy peers

1.6.1   Asthma

Many studies have documented the association between asthma and psychiatric problems, with most investigations suggesting that children and adolescents with asthma are at increased risk for anxiety and depression (Forero, Bauman, Young, Booth, & Nutbeam, 1996; Wamboldt, Fritz, Mansell, McQuaid, & Klein, 1998). However, the literature is not entirely consistent regarding psychological problems in children with asthma, with some recent studies indicating no heightened risk for depression (Bender, Annett, Ikle, DuHamel, Rand, & Strunk, 2000). In fact, a recent meta-analysis on 26 studies of behavioral adjustment in children with asthma found that these children generally show more behavioral problems relative to their healthy peers, especially internalizing disorders (e.g., anxiety, depression; McQuaid, Kopel, &Nassau, 2001). They also found that greater asthma severity was associated with a higher frequency of behavioral difficulties. The authors conclude that children with asthma, particularly the severe type, should be considered at higher risk for behavioral difficulties that may require psychosocial intervention.

Children with asthma may be at a higher risk for behavioral difficulties

1.6.2   Cancer

The evidence is equivocal as to whether children undergoing treatment for cancer are at greater risk for experiencing psychosocial adjustment problems relative to their healthy peers. For example, studies have reported some difficulties in social adjustment with peers (Katz, Rubinstein, Hubert, & Blew, 1988; Larcombe, Walker, Charlton, Meller, Jones, & Mott, 1991), and with emotional well-being (Bennett, 1994; Varni, Katz, Colegrove, & Dolgin, 1995) among children being treated for cancer. However, more recent studies that have examined social functioning, emotional well-being, and behavioral functioning have failed to provide any differences in psychosocial functioning between children with cancer and their healthy peers (Noll, Gartstein, Vannatta, Correll, Bukowski, & Davies, 1999; Eiser, Hill, & Vance, 2000). Indeed, it has been suggested that the majority of children with cancer function similarly to healthy comparison peers without cancer, after returning to school (Noll et al., 1999) or at one-year postdiagnosis (Sawyer, Antoniou, Toogood, & Rice, 1997). This finding suggests considerable psychological hardiness among this population. Other investigators have proposed that children who have survived cancer are at greater risk for posttraumatic stress disorder, although the data have generally suggested a subthreshold of symptoms and not enough symptoms to warrant a full diagnosis of posttraumatic stress disorder.

1.6.3   Cystic Fibrosis

Simmons and Goldberg (2001) reviewed the literature on infants and preschoolers with cystic fibrosis (CF) and concluded that these children generally evidence adequate psychological adjustment, although a small minority of children is at a higher risk for insecure attachment. The evidence on the psychological adjustment of school-age children and adolescents with CF is decidedly mixed. While some investigators have reported relatively typical adjustment among child and adolescent CF patients (Czyzewski & Bartholomew, 1998; Pumariega, Pearson, & Seilheimer, 1993), others have suggested elevated levels of anxiety, somatic complaints, and behavioral disturbances (Thompson, Gustafson, Gill, Godfrey, & Bennett-Murphy, 1998; Thompson, Gustafson, Hamlett, & Spock, 1992). Finally, several investigations have reported that these symptoms may be transient, as many children demonstrate improved functioning over time (Thompson, Gustafson, Gil, Kinney, & Spock, 1999; Wilson, Fosson, Kanga, & D'Angelo, 1996).

1.6.4   Diabetes Mellitus

The body of evidence on the psychological adjustment among children and adolescents with diabetes indicates that they are at increased risk for depression, anxiety, and eating disorders (Wysocki et al., 2003), with many youth experiencing adjustment problems soon after the diagnosis of diabetes (Jacobson, Hauser, Wertlieb, Woldsdorf, Orleans, & Viegra, 1986). For example, one study of adolescents with type I diabetes reported that over 30% of these youth evidenced criteria for a psychiatric disorder, with the majority involving internalizing symptoms (Blanz, Rensch-Riemann, Fritz-Sigmund, & Schmidt, 1993). Specifically, the adolescents with diabetes reported more somatic symptoms, sleeping disturbances, compulsions, and depressive moods when compared to their healthy counterparts. Moreover, eating disorders are reported to be approximately twice as common in adolescent females with type I diabetes as in their peers without diabetes (Jones, Lawson, Daneman, Olmstead, & Rodin, 2000). It also should be noted that behavioral problems are more apparent among adolescents than younger children, which in turn increases problems with disease self-management and glycemic control.

Children with diabetes are at increased risk for depression, anxiety, and eating disorders

1.6.5   Sickle Cell Disease

Research indicates that sickle cell disease (SCD) is a particular risk factor for the development of psychiatric disorders, especially depression and anxiety, in children and adolescents (Garstein et al., 1999; Thompson et al., 1998). For example, adolescents with SCD have shown significantly less body satisfaction and higher levels of depressive symptoms when compared to their healthy peers (Morgan & Jackson, 1986). Another study found more depressive symptoms based on self-reports, higher levels of internalizing symptoms based on mothers' reports, and higher levels of externalizing symptoms based on teachers' reports among children with SCD in comparison to their sibling controls (Brown, Doepke, & Kaslow, 1993).

1.7   Diagnostic Procedures and Documentation

Because a child with a chronic illness may have primary or secondary psychological or neurological problems, a targeted assessment that evaluates domains of behavior, cognition, and affect, among other important functional areas, represents a standard means by which children and adolescents are evaluated for a psychiatric diagnosis or neurological impairment. Assessment tools that evaluate any child psychiatric symptoms may be chosen based on their ability to describe the characteristics and impact of the presenting issues accurately (Mortweet & Christophersen, 2003). Therefore, a multivariate approach to assessment including child and caregiver interviews, direct observations of behavior, and rating scales, each of which are gathered in multiple settings, is a best-practice approach when assessing children's adjustment and adaptation to chronic illness. Ideally, these ratings should come from multiple sources, including teachers, parents, peers, and the children themselves across a variety of settings and situations, because each of these informants provides a unique perspective (Klinnert, McQuaid, McCormick, Adinoff, & Bryant, 2000). For a thorough review of objective tests, diagnostic criteria, and diagnostic procedures, the reader is referred to Chapter 3 (Diagnosis and Treatment Indications).

2

Theories and Models of the Disorder

Conceptually-based, theoretically-driven models that predict adaptation of children to a chronic illness and their families have only been present for the past two decades. These theoretical and conceptual models view chronic illness as a potential stressor requiring adaptation. The two prominent models that have been proposed are: the transactional stress and coping (TSC) model (Thompson & Gustafson, 1996) and the disability stress coping (DSC) model (Wallander, Varni, Babani, Banis, & Wilcox, 1989). These theoretical models provide a useful framework for conceptualizing the interrelationships of biomedical factors, psychosocial factors, coping, and managing stress, all of which are believed to predict adaptation. In general, both theoretical models imply that psychosocial factors serve as potential protective mechanisms by buffering the impact of the stressor (e.g., medical severity) on overall adaptation to the stressors associated with illness. Both models are based on variants of systems theory which posits: (a) that systems are composed of interrelated parts, (b) that change in one part is associated with change in all other parts, (c) that systems maintain a regular state of balance, and finally, (d) that systems maintain a balance in periods of stability and change (Hoffman, 1981).

> The two most prominent models for adaptation of children to a chronic illness include the transactional stress and coping model and the disability stress coping model

The TSC model is grounded within an ecological-systems theory perspective whereby chronic illness is viewed as a potential stressor to which the individual and family system attempt to adapt. The model conceptualizes a relationship between chronic illness and adaptation that varies as a function of biomedical, developmental, and psychosocial systems. The illness-adjustment relationship is a function of the transactions of three broad components included in the model: (a) disease and disability parameters, including disease type, duration of illness, and severity of symptoms; (b) child and demographic parameters including age, gender, and socio-economic status (SES); and (c) psychosocial processes such as stress, coping, and family functioning.

In the TSC model, the following three adaptational processes affect the child's psychosocial adjustment above and beyond the contributions of the illness and family demographic variables:

1. Cognitive processes in children and parents, such as stress appraisal, expectations of treatment efficacy, and self-esteem and health locus of control.
2. Methods of coping used by children and parents including palliative coping or adaptive coping. Palliative coping includes a combination of avoidance, wishful thinking, and emotion-focused coping. Adaptive coping, or problem-focused coping, involves altering the stressful transaction between the environment and person by attempting to change the environment or the self.

3. Types of family functioning are categorized as supportive, conflicted, or controlling.

These adaptational processes are the proposed mediators of the illness and adjustment relationship. This transactional stress and coping model places a significant emphasis on maternal psychological adjustment and any direct effects it may have on the psychological adaptation of children with various chronic illnesses. Interestingly, illness severity and family demographic factors, in turn, account for a rather small percentage of the variance in mother and child adaptation to illness. In following this model, the goals of treatment include altering cognitive appraisals, coping methods, and family functioning that serve to reduce stress related to tasks associated with illness and environmental transactions. Successful adaptation is posited to be reflected in health and adherence as well as in psychosocial adjustment.

The DSC model proposes another framework from which to consider multiple biopsychosocial characteristics and their overall influence on psychological adjustment to a childhood chronic illness or disability. This model was developed from Wallander and colleagues' interest in explaining the wide variation in the psychosocial adjustment and adaptation of children with chronic diseases. Risk and resilience variables are the organizing framework for this model and are purported to mediate and moderate the relationship between disability stress and adjustment. In the DSC model, stress is believed to be the variable primarily responsible for elevating the risk of psychosocial problems (Wallander et al., 1989).

Characteristics associated with the disability or disease, the child, and the child's social environment are identified as either risk or resistance factors. Risk factors include:

Risk factors include illness parameters, functional independence level or adaptation, and psychosocial stressors

1. Illness parameters such as the type of diagnosis the child has received, the duration of the disease or disability, the visibility and severity of the condition, and the degree of central nervous system involvement or neurological impairment.
2. Functional independence level or adaptation of the individual in daily activities.
3. Psychosocial stressors factors related to living with a disability, major life events, and daily hassles.

Key protective or resistance factors are separated into three categories:

Protective or resistance factors include intrapersonal factors, social-ecological factors, and stress-processing factors

1. Intrapersonal factors that refer to fairly stable personality characteristics such as temperament, problem-solving abilities, motivation, or sense of self.
2. Social-ecological factors that include socio-economic status (SES), parental adjustment, familial resources, family functioning, and social support.
3. Stress-processing factors which refer to health locus of control, stress appraisal, and coping strategies.

Wallander's model proposes that the complex interactions of these risk and resistance factors account for the child or adolescent's overall adjustment to the chronic illness. For example, when children experience increased stress associated with their condition (e.g., worsening illness or some loss of functional independence), these circumstances may increase the effects of psychosocial stressors already experienced by children. As a result, adjustment problems may develop. However, children with an adequate number of protective or resistance factors may be less vulnerable to psychosocial adjustment problems and may be more likely to evidence optimal adaptation to their chronic illness. Therefore, identifying modifiable risk and resistance factors will prove critical when developing new interventions for youth with a chronic illness. In accordance with this model, the goal of treatment is to reduce risk factors and increase resistance factors.

The TSC model and DSC model address many of the same risk and protective variables purported to influence children's adaptation to a chronic illness. Risk factors for both models include psychosocial stressors and disability/disease parameters. Both models also identify socioecological variables (e.g., external support), intrapersonal factors, and stress processing (i.e., ways of coping) as resistance factors. For example, appropriate adaptational processes from the TSC model are similar to the resistance factors from the DCS model in that the more appropriate the processes, the less vulnerable a child is to maladjustment. More importantly, such factors also are likely to predict resiliency.

Although the transactional stress and coping model and the DSC model represent the two prominent models in the extant literature, there have been additional models to examine children and adolescents adaptation to chronic illness within a family context and from a developmental perspective. For example, Kazak, Alderfer, Rourke, Simms, Streisand, & Grossman. (2004) conceptualized chronic illness or disability as a specific stressor or trauma that exerts particular influences on the developing child, the family, or specific subsystems within the family, such as siblings.

Insufficient attention has been provided for the role of general developmental processes as salient features in the conceptualizations of adjustment for children and adolescents with chronic disease or disability (Wallander et al., 2003). Inclusion of developmental constructs is particularly important in these models given that children and adolescents are developing organisms. In addition, the systems in which they interact, such as the family, also experience significant developmental milestones and critical periods in their development (Wallander et al., 2003). Therefore, greater research efforts need to focus on longitudinal designs, the course of the disease or illness, and its management. Finally, the interaction of the disease, the child's developmental course, and the family (Wallander et al., 2003) needs to be considered.

Given the host of stressors associated with any chronic illness, research has focused on investigating those factors that best predict positive adaptation to the disease process for children experiencing a variety of chronic conditions. In addition, researchers have proposed that the different adaptational processes employed by the child and family may mediate the relation between chronic illness and psychological adjustment. The existing body of research associated with these models has made a substantial contribution by identifying psychosocial variables associated with variability in adaptation.

2.1   Risk Factors

Psychological risk is multidimensional, and it is influenced by many factors that can complicate disease presentations and management (Wallander &

Thompson, 1995). These factors include severity of disease, biological and genetic risk factors, environmental influences, decreased competency in daily living activities, and psychosocial stressors.

2.1.1   Disease and Disability Parameters

Disease and disability parameters are biological dimensions that combine to cause disease, exacerbate severity of disease, and influence children's overall adjustment to disease. Biological risk factors include genetically based disorders (e.g., cystic fibrosis, Down's syndrome), teratogens that result in disabilities (e.g., alcohol, tobacco, cocaine), and congenital disorders (e.g., congenital heart disease).

2.1.2   Genetic Disorders

Many chronic diseases are genetically based and result from either a chromosomal abnormality or more subtle genetic defects that may influence key biological processes (Thompson & Gustafson, 1996). Evidence indicates that 3–5% of children are born with some form of a congenital malformation (Berry, Buehler, Strauss, Hogue, & Smith, 1987). Autosomal recessive patterns represent the most common chromosomal abnormality, and they are characterized by the child inheriting a disease-causing gene from each parent. Sickle cell disease and cystic fibrosis are common examples of autosomal recessive genetic disorders.

2.1.3   Intrauterine Growth Retardation, Prematurity, and Low Birth Weight

Low birth weight (< 2500 grams) frequently results from intrauterine growth retardation, prematurity (< 37 weeks gestational age), or both. Children with low birth rate account for 7.4% of births (Aylward, 2003). Although recent medical technological advances have improved survival rates of children with low birth weight, these children nonetheless are at particular risk for multiple health problems (McCormick, 1985). Variables related to low birth rate include poor nutrition and low maternal weight gain during pregnancy, maternal infections, smoking, prenatal drug abuse, and poor access to and use of prenatal care programs (Institute of Medicine, 1988). Children with very low birth weights are at risk for mental retardation and other learning problems with visual-motor skills, school/learning difficulties, and behavioral issues (e.g., ADHD) (see, Aylward, 2003).

2.1.4   Teratogens

Teratogens are substances transferred from the mother to the developing fetus that can cause systemic malformations and other structural defects. Alcohol, opiates, (e.g., heroin, methadone), cocaine, anticonvulsant medications (e.g., phenobarbital, phenytoin, valproic acid), and lead are extensively studied teratogens that affect CNS development. Alcohol is a potent teratogen in infants, and prenatal alcohol exposure is unequivocally associated with birth defects, developmental disabilities, and cognitive and behavioral difficulties. Prenatal drug abuse, including cocaine, opiates, and other drugs also may affect the CNS functioning of the drug-exposed infant (Chasnoff, Griffith, Freier, & Murray, 1992).

2.1.5   Disease Severity

It is unclear if there is an association between severity of disease and psychological adaptation. Data indicate that disease severity increases the risk of psychological problems in children with renal disease (Garralda, Jameson, Reynolds, & Postlethwaite, 1988; Isao & Hiroko 1995). Specifically, children receiving dialysis in a hospital were at greater risk for psychological problems than both those receiving dialysis at home and posttransplant children (Brownbridge & Fielding, 1991). In contrast, no differences were found in self-reported anxiety of children with severe asthma versus children with mild or moderate asthma (Wamboldt et al., 1998). Two reviews found that disease severity was associated with increased risk for psychological adjustment difficulties (Lavigne & Faier-Routman, 1992; McQuaid et al., 2001), whereas a review by Bennett (1994) reported that depression was inconsistently related to severity of disease. These studies may be confounded because few research diagnostic criteria exist for quantifying severity of disease among various chronic illnesses.

2.1.6   Functional Independence

Functional independence or functional capacity is determined by competencies in activities of daily living. Although few studies have investigated the impact of functional independence on the adaptive behaviors of children with chronic illness, emerging evidence suggests that functional independence is linked to whether the child is going to cope or adjust well to their illness. Children whose activities are restricted, either socially or physically, are more likely to have difficulties coping. Children who have more absences from school also are more likely to evidence a poor psychological adjustment (Weitzman, 1986). In contrast, higher adaptive functioning is associated with younger children, girls, and greater intellectual functioning (Brown, Eckman, Baldwin, Buchanan, & Dingle, 1995).

Children who are frequently absent from school may demonstrate poor psychological adjustment

2.1.7   Psychosocial Stressors

Psychosocial stressors include illness-related difficulties, major life events, and daily stressors. Illness-related difficulties refer to the sequelae of the disease or trauma, including stress resulting from school absenteeism or limitations from activities that require physical exertion. A child's illness and treatment regimen may be stressors that deplete the child's environmental or interpersonal resources, thereby resulting in impaired psychosocial functioning. Major life events consist of major external changes, either positive or negative. Daily stressors are minor annoyances or daily hassles that occur during the course of a typical day. As applied to chronic illness, daily stressors may include the presence of physical symptoms such as pain and fatigue and tasks that need to be completed for effective disease management (e.g., taking prescribed medication).

High levels of stress increase the risk for adjustment problems such as depression or anxiety

Previous studies of children with a chronic illness have demonstrated that high stress increases the risk for adjustment problems, such as anxiety and depression (Varni, Katz, Colegrove, & Dolgin, 1994; Varni, Setoguchi, Rappaport, & Talbot, 1991). For example, cancer survivors who experienced illness-related difficulties, such as restrictions in activities or severe cosmetic changes, demonstrated more depressive symptoms than the survivors who did not share these experiences (Greenberg, Kazak, & Meadows, 1989). In addition, LeBovidge, Lavigne, and Miller (2005) examined the relationship

Table 4
Biopsychosocial Organizational Framework

Dimension	Asthma	Cancer	CF	DM	SCD	SB
Etiology						
Genetic			X		X	
Nongenetic	X	X		X		X
Age of Onset						
Birth			X		X	X
Childhood	X	X		X		
Course						
Static						X
Episodic	X					
Progressive				X	X	
Fatal		?	X			
Impairment						
Cognitive		X		?	X	X
Motor					X	X
Visible		X	X		X	X
Medical Regimen						
Pills	X	X	X	X	X	
Injection		X		X		
Inhalants	X		X			
Physical therapy or exercise			X	X		
Diet			X	X		

Note: CF=cystic fibrosis, DM=diabetes mellitus, SCD=sickle cell disease, SB=spina bifida. From Thompson & Gustafson (1996). Reprinted with permission.

of psychosocial stress and attitude toward illness to psychological adjustment among youth with chronic arthritis. Higher levels of illness-related and nonill-ness-related stress were associated with higher levels of anxiety and depressive symptoms and parent-reported adjustment problems. A direct association between stress from negative major life events and adjustment problems among youth with a chronic illness has also been demonstrated (Timko, Stovel, Baumgartner, & Moos, 1995; von Weiss et al., 2002). In addition, fewer reports of daily hassles predicated fewer adjustment problems in children with pediatric rheumatoid diseases (von Weiss et al., 2002). These findings support earlier findings demonstrating that the stress associated with daily hassles and the use of avoidance coping account for much of the variance in children's adaptation to the disease process (Thompson & Gustafson, 1996).

2.2 Resistance Factors

2.2.1 Intrapersonal Factors

Intrapersonal factors include the child's temperament, social and academic competence, motivation, self-esteem, and problem-solving abilities. These characteristics may influence a child's adaptation to a chronic illness in combination with disease and disability factors and family variables and are associated with psychosocial adjustment. The effect of children's competence on maladjustment has been documented in the literature for chronic illnesses such as sickle cell disease (Casey, Brown, & Bakeman, 2000), congenital heart defects (Casey, Sykes, Craig, Power, & Mulholland, 1996), and brain tumors (Radcliffe, Bennett, Kazak, Foley, & Phillips, 1996). Findings also indicate a relationship between internal health locus of control and child adaptation (Brown, Davis, Lambert, Hsu, Hopkins, & Eckman, 2000). In an examination of children's ability to manage their chronic disease, higher intrapersonal scores predicted a greater frequency of subsequent visits to the physician to follow-up an episode of asthma symptoms (Clark, Gong, & Kaciroti, 2001). Bauman, Drotar, Leventhal, Perrin, & Pless (1997) conducted a review of psychosocial interventions for children with chronic health conditions and found nine studies that assessed self-esteem, self-efficacy, or social competence. Four of the nine studies demonstrated significant improvement on these variables while one study demonstrated improvement on locus of control, and another showed improvement on family functioning.

2.3 Social-Ecological Factors

2.3.1 Family Functioning

Social-ecological factors include the family environment and family members' adaptation, social support systems, and family utilitarian resources (e.g., intact, divorced, presence of siblings, family income and health care financ-

Positive family functioning is associated with better psychological adaptation for children with a chronic illness

ing, parental responsibilities and leisure time, parental education level). The family environment and its level of functioning accounts for a significant role in predicting adaptation to chronic illness among children and their caregivers (Thompson et al., 1999). In one investigation that examined factors influencing adolescent's adaptation to sickle cell disease, parent- and adolescent-rated family relations accounted for a significant amount of variance associated with rates of self-reported anxiety and depression (Burlew, Telfair, Colangelo, & Wright, 2000). A longitudinal design was used to evaluate the relations between maternal-rated family functioning and maternal-rated adjustment problems in a sample of children with sickle cell disease over a two year period. A reciprocal association was found between family functioning and behavior problems. Specifically, an increase in behavior problems was associated with an increase in family conflict, whereas higher baseline levels of family conflict increased the risk of behavior problems throughout the course of the study. Family cohesiveness and family support are also important factors that directly influence children's adjustment to a chronic illness (Ievers, Brown, Lambert, Hsu, & Eckman, 1998). A review by Hocking & Lochman (2005) provides support for the importance of family functioning in child adjustment, specifically as applied to sickle cell disease and insulin-dependent diabetes mellitus. As expected, greater adaptive family relationships and parental psychological adjustment are positively associated with better psychological adaptation for children with a chronic illness (Drotar, 1997).

2.3.2   Financial Resources

Poverty is a significant risk factor for poor management of chronic illness in children. The association between poverty and poor disease management has been attributed to a lack of resources, a diminished ability to obtain existing services, and the lack of appropriate adherence necessary to manage complicated disease regimens. There is a strong association between children's health problems and poverty (see Tarnowski, Brown, & Simonian, 1999), and there is evidence to suggest that children with a chronic illness from poor families are inadequately served by our existing health care system (Newacheck, 1994).

2.3.3   Stress Processing

Stress processing consists of coping strategy variables, attitudes toward illness, locus of control, and cognitive appraisal. Coping strategies typically have been conceptualized as adaptive, active, or engagement types of coping, but also include avoidance or disengagement coping. Meijer, Sinnema, Bijstra, Mellenbergh, and Wolters (2002) examined coping styles and locus of control as predictors of psychological adjustment of adolescents with a chronic illness. Coping styles described as "seeking social support" and "confrontation" predicted positive social adjustment, whereas the coping style "depression" predicted poor adjustment resulting from low social self-esteem and high social anxiety. Avoidance coping and locus of control were not strongly associated with psychosocial adjustment. However, in a similar study that investigated coping strategies, child adaptation was associated with an internal health locus of control (Brown et al., 2000). Children who engage in negative thinking and passive strategies in order to cope with their illness are less active in school and social situations, and demonstrate a greater frequency of psychological problems, compared to children who engage in active coping strategies (Gil, Williams, Thompson, & Kinney, 1991).

Thompson and colleagues (1998) examined adjustment and cognitive adaptational process in children with cystic fibrosis and sickle cell disease. Significant portions of the variance in adjustment were accounted for by stress appraisal (19%), expectations of efficacy (9%), and health locus of control (9%) for children with cystic fibrosis, and by stress appraisal (21%) and self-worth (12%) for children with sickle cell disease. A study that assessed the cognitive coping strategies of children with chronic illnesses reported active coping as their predominant strategy for adapting to common painful and stressful events (Olson, Johansen, Powers, Pope, & Klein, 1993). Overall, research affirms the importance of adaptive coping in predicting adjustment for children with chronic illnesses (Brown & Macias, 2001).

Adaptive coping may help the adjustment process for children with chronic illnesses

2.4   Applying the Models to Sickle Cell Disease

In this section we review the two models, the disability stress coping (DSC) model and the transactional stress and coping (TSC) model, as they apply to understanding the interaction of illness and adjustment in children and adolescents with sickle cell disease. As described previously, sickle cell disease (SCD) is a chronic hematological condition characterized by debilitating pain episodes, stroke, anemia, and major organ failure, as well as other serious complications. Medical management of SCD is life-long and often requires routine clinic appointments, emergency room visits, and frequent hospitalizations.

In the first example, we describe the application of the DSC model for understanding the complex interaction of biological, psychological, and social factors affecting children's overall psychological adjustment to SCD. Employing the risk-resistance adaptation model, Casey et al. (2000) examined the impact of risk and resistance factors on the psychological adjustment of 118 children and adolescents with SCD receiving treatment at a comprehensive sickle cell center. Assessments included risk factors (condition parameters, functional independence, and disability stressors), resistance factors (stress processing, intrapersonal factors, and social ecological factors), and adjustment. Adaptive behavior was associated with child maladjustment such that less adaptive competency as demonstrated by the child was associated with a higher frequency of difficulties. In addition, severity of disease was associated with disability stress, and child competence was associated with child maladjustment. The results suggest that increasing child competence may diminish the level of adjustment difficulties in children with SCD. Coping did not moderate the association between stress and child maladjustment. Finally, adaptive behavior and stress did not mediate the association between severity of disability and maladjustment, as the model had predicted.

In a follow-up study that only included children and adolescents with SCD and not their families, Brown et al. (2000) investigated risk and resistance factors for children with sickle cell syndromes disease and their primary caregivers. Measures included adjustment (i.e., primary caregiver and child adjustment), risk factors (i.e., disease and disability, functional independence, and psychosocial stressors), resistance factors (i.e., intrapersonal health locus of control, social-ecological), and stress processing (coping). Primary caregivers' adjustment was associated with developmental coping, and child adaptation was associated with an internal health locus of control. As well, an indirect effect of primary caregivers' coping on child adjustment was found through influence on primary caregivers' adjustment.

The TSC model differs from the DSC model in that it places greater emphasis on maternal adaptational processes as they relate to children's adjustment to their illness. In a recent investigation involving maternal cognitive processes, mothers with generally adequate adjustment had lower levels of daily stress and illness-related stress, whereas significant decrements in maternal adjustment over time were associated with high levels of daily stress (Thompson et al., 1999). Poor maternal adjustment has been associated with low use of adaptive coping and higher rates of palliative coping (e.g., emotion-focused coping, avoidance, wishful thinking) when examining maternal methods of coping (Thompson et al., 1999). Family functioning may also have a direct impact on child adjustment, in contrast to being part of the maternal mediational processes that affect maternal adjustment as posited in the TSC model (Hocking & Lochman, 2005). For example, conflicted family functioning accounted for a significant amount of the variance in mother-reported behavior problems in children with SCD (Thompson et al., 1999), while parent and adolescent rated family relations accounted for a significant portion of the variance in rates of depression and anxiety in children and adolescents with SCD (Burlew et al., 2000). In a recent longitudinal study, an increase in behavior problems for children with SCD was associated with an increase in family conflict, while the risk of consistent behavior problems was associated with higher baseline levels of family conflict (Thompson, Armstrong, Link, Pegelow, Moser, & Wang, 2003).

Investigations of cognitive processes for child adaptation have shown that lower levels of self-worth are associated with higher rates of depression and anxiety among children with SCD (Burlew et al., 2000; Thompson et al., 1999). Investigations that have examined health locus of control have failed to find an association with adjustment (Thompson, Gil, Burbach, Keith, & Kinney, 1993; Thompson, Gustafson, George, & Spock, 1994; Thompson et al., 1998; Thompson et al., 1999).

Active coping strategies among children with SCD have been associated with reports of lower levels of pain during a laboratory pain task (Gil, Shand, Fuggle, Dugan, & Davies, 1997). Avoidance coping also has been positively associated with greater levels of anxiety (Lewis & Kliewer, 1996), while high levels of disengagement coping have been associated with higher levels of mothers' ratings of their children's adjustment (Casey et al., 2000). Negative thinking also has been associated with higher levels of child-reported problems (Thompson et al., 1993). In addition, children who engaged in fewer coping attempts and more negative thinking experienced significant adjustment difficulties (Thompson, et al., 1999). Overall, the existing empirical evidence suggests that child and general family factors are more important in predicting child adjustment than are maternal adaptational processes and maternal adjustment (Hocking & Lochman, 2005).

Diagnosis and Treatment Indications

A multivariate
approach is best for
assessing children's
psychosocial
adjustment and
adaptation to chronic
illness

As mentioned earlier, a best-practice approach when assessing children's psychosocial adjustment and adaptation to chronic illness includes a multivariate approach to assessment that includes child and caregiver interviews, direct observations of behavior, and subjective and objective rating scales, each of which are gathered in multiple settings. It is noteworthy, however, that few assessment instruments have been systematically normed for children and adolescents with a chronic illness. While the majority of the behavior and emotional measures typically employed in the pediatric illness literature have sound reliability, validity, and standardized norms, the standardization samples for these instruments have primarily been based on child psychopathology rather than chronic illness. Further, the theoretical framework that has guided the development of these instruments has been based almost exclusively on a model of psychopathology. Therefore, when interpreting data from these instruments in clinical practice, there are inherent challenges given the common overlap between many medical and psychiatric symptoms as well as iatrogenic treatment effects for medical problems.

A child with cancer being treated with chemotherapy may experience a lack of energy and sleep disturbances. Although these are two primary symptoms of depression, they also are adverse effects associated with chemotherapy or radiation therapy (the most common treatments for cancer), and should not be confused with a depressive disorder. Nonetheless, scores for a child with these symptoms on a rating scale that is primarily symptom-driven may indicate clinically significant problems with depression. Therefore, the astute practitioner, through examination of all available evidence, must determine whether the presenting symptoms are secondary to the chronic illness or whether they actually represent a psychiatric disorder or perhaps a cluster of symptoms that may eventually result in a psychiatric disorder. Overall, no specific assessment battery exists for children with chronic illness. Brief descriptions of the various methods used to assess behavioral, cognitive, and affective functioning of youth with a chronic illness are presented in the following sections. In addition, measures that assess adherence, stress and coping, quality of life, and family variables are reviewed.

3.1 Caregiver and Child Interviews

Caregiver and child interviews often represent the initial step when evaluating adjustment, adaptation, coping, and quality of life in youth with a chronic illness. Important information gathered from these interviews will likely include historical and current information that aids in conceptualizing the presenting problem. Current information gathered from the interview can include the child's age, gender, and family socioeconomic status. Because family functioning represents an important component of the transactional stress and coping model as well as the disability stress coping model, caregiver interviews provide important information about family relationships and the level of family support, all of which may predict adaptation to the chronic illness. Open-ended questions about family strengths and weakness elicit valuable information about how well the family functions as a unit, the family resources they may possess, and how they cope and adapt with those stressors associated with their child's chronic illness.

3.2   Behavior

Techniques to assess behaviors among children and adolescents include the use of direct observations of behavior, rating scales of behavior that may be completed by self-assessment from the child or adolescent, by caregiver's and teacher's ratings, and sociometric ratings completed by peers. Direct observations typically entail observations of children's behavior in a clinical or laboratory setting, playroom, classroom, or home setting. Behavior rating scales are widely used in the clinical diagnosis of children with various types of psychopathology. Standardized rating scales are typically administered to teachers, parents, and, in the case of some instruments, the children or adolescents themselves. Parent and teacher rating scales are particularly valuable for assessing behaviors of children as they provide a general summary of behavior across a period of time such as several days or even weeks. Rating scales also are useful for monitoring the effectiveness of a treatment program. This is due, in part, to the fact that rating scales provide avenues for assessing similar symptoms across several settings (e.g., school and home) and at different times of the day. In addition, rating scales can provide a way for ongoing and repeated assessments during and after treatment and to determine the effect of any changes that may be associated with various treatments or specific medication.

Rating scales are an important assessment tool for evaluating behavior

The most commonly used behavior rating scales for children and adolescents are the Conners Parent and Teacher Rating Scales (Conners, 1997), the Child Behavior Checklist (CBCL; Achenbach, 1991), and the Behavior Assessment Rating Scale (BASC; Reynolds & Kamphaus, 1992). These aforementioned rating scales have been used primarily for assessment of symptoms of psychopathology. The primary advantages of rating scales include simplicity in administration and scoring, cost-effectiveness, and reduced subjectivity (see Brown, Dingle, & Dreelin, 1997). However, if more diagnostic information is needed, a structured interview, such as the Child Assessment Schedule (Hodges, Kline, Stern, Cytryn, & McKnew, 1982), the Diagnostic Interview Schedule for Children (DISC-IV; Shaffer, Fisher, Lucas, Dulcan, & Schwab-Stone, 2000), or a semistructured interview, such as the Semistructured Clinical Interview for Children and Adolescents (SCICA; McConaughy & Achenbach, 1994), may prove useful. Finally, the Pediatric Symptom Checklist (PSC; Jellinek et al., 1999) is a psychosocial screening instrument designed to facilitate the screening and recognition of cognitive, emotional, and behavioral problems in children and adolescents that can be used in pediatric primary care settings.

3.3   Cognition

Cognitive processes represent an important factor in the transactional stress and coping model, whereas the degree of central nervous system involvement or neurological impairment are factors included in the disability stress coping model. Cognitive targets for assessment may include general intellectual abilities; educational levels; specific knowledge concerning illness and treatment; attitudes toward health and illness, and health care providers; perceived threat of illness; perceived control over psychological and physical symptoms; perception of costs and benefits of possible treatment regimens; and expectations about future outcomes (Belar & Deardorff, 1995). The central nervous system (CNS) functioning in children with a chronic illness may be affected depending on the illness itself or the iatrogenic effects of the treatment employed for the management of the illness (Brown, 2006). Disruption of functioning in the CNS may influence cognition, learning, or emotional functioning that in turn affects classroom or academic performance. The most common measures of cognitive function for children and adolescents include the Wechsler Preschool and Primary Scale of Intelligence – Third Edition (Wechsler, 2002), the Wechsler Intelligence Scale for Children – Fourth Edition (Wechsler, 2003), and the Stanford-Binet Intelligence Scale – Fifth Edition (Roid, 2003). Instruments that assess academic achievement include the Wide Range Achievement Test – Third Edition (Stone, Jastak, & Wilkinson, 1995), the Wechsler Individual Achievement Test – Second Edition (The Psychological Corporation, 2001), and the Woodcock-Johnson Tests of Academic Achievement – Third Edition (Woodcock, McGrew, & Mather, 2001).

For children and adolescents with a chronic illness, attitude toward illness, locus of control, and attributional style (i.e., how an individual accounts for the causes of positive and negative events) also are important cognitive variables. The Illness Attitude Scale (Eminson, Benjamin, Shortall, Woods, & Faragher, 1996) assesses children's attitudes and degree of concern about illness and health. The Children's Health Locus of Control Scale (CHLC; Parcel & Meyer, 1978) assesses children's locus of control pertaining to aspects of health and illness. Finally, children's and adolescents' attributional style may be assessed with the Children's Attributional Style Questionnaire (CASQ; Kaslow, Tannenbaum, & Seligman, 1978).

3.4   Affect

Examining children's and adolescents' affective functioning is important because of the association between emotional functioning and adherence and disease adaptation. Self-report rating scales to screen for emotional difficulties in children and adolescents include the Children's Depression Inventory (CDI; Kovacs, 1992), the Beck Depression Inventory for Youth (BDI-Y; Beck, Beck, & Jolly, 2001), the Revised Children's Manifest Anxiety Scale (RCMAS; Reynolds & Richmond, 1978), and the State-Trait Anxiety Inventory for Children (STAIC; Spielberger, Edwards, Lushene, Monuori, & Platzek, 1973). The Personal Adjustment and Roles Skills Scale (PARS III; Stein & Jessop, 1990) is a parent-rated measure of the psychological adjustment of children and adolescents with disabilities or chronic illnesses. Although the PARS is a screening instrument rather than a diagnostic instrument, children who score below the recommended cutoff score are likely to meet diagnostic criteria for an emotional or behavioral disorder (Harris, Canning, & Kelleher, 1996). Scores from the PARS and CBCL are highly correlated (Harris et al., 1996).

Self-report rating scales can be used to screen for emotional difficulties in children and adolescents

3.5 Adherence

Rating scales and parent reports are also used to assess adherence to treatment and may be completed by caregivers and children. Similar to behavioral rating scales, scales that measure adherence are easy to administer, cost-effective, and can assess a complex array of behaviors (e.g., amount and timing of meals, frequency and duration of exercise) (La Greca & Bearman, 2003). Most measures of adherence generally overestimate adherence and obtaining an accurate assessment of adherence from typically nonadherent youngsters is challenging (La Greca & Bearman, 2003). Self-report measures of adherence tend to be more accurate when they involve a short recall period (e.g., 24 hours) and solicit detailed objective information (La Greca & Bearman, 2003). Examples of pediatric self-report adherence regimen questionnaires include the Self-Care Inventory (SCI), that assesses perceived adherence to diabetes regimens across several aspects of diabetes care (La Greca, Follansbee, & Skyler, 1990), and the Treatment Adherence Questionnaire-CF (TAQ-CF, DiGirolamo, Quittner, Ackerman, & Stevens, 1997), which assesses adherence behaviors in both adolescents with cystic fibrosis and their parents. Additional methods of measuring adherence include drug assays, ratings by health professionals, behavioral observations, pill counts, and electronic monitoring devices.

3.6 Stress and Coping

Methods of coping (e.g., active and palliative) are included in the transactional stress and coping model, whereas stress-processing factors such as stress appraisal and coping strategies are mainstays of the disability stress coping model. Stress levels for children and adolescents with a chronic illness have been evaluated with the UCLA Life Stress Interview for Children: Chronic Stress and Episodic Life Events (Hammen & Rudolph, 1999), which is a semistructured interview that assesses chronic stress and episodic stress.

One widely used instrument for evaluating children's and adolescent's coping strategies is the Kidcope (Spirito, Stark, & Williams, 1988), which is a checklist designed to assess cognitive, emotional, and social coping strategies. Additional coping measures for children and adolescents include the Children's Coping Strategies Checklist (Sandler, Tein, & West, 1994), the child version of the Coping Strategies Inventory (CSI; Tobin, Holroyd, & Reynolds, 1989), and the Ways of Coping Questionnaire (Folkman & Lazarus, 1988).

3.7   Quality of Life

Given the recent advances in medical care, issues of quality of life are an important aspect of chronic illness in children and adolescents. Assessment of quality of life may include evaluating the degree of functional impairment caused by a chronic illness, and whether the illness affects school, social, and personal adjustment. Generic quality of life assessment measures include the Quality of Well-Being Scale (QWB; Kaplan, Anderson, Wu, Mathews, Kozin, & Orenstein, 1989), and the Child Health Questionnaire (CHQ; Landgraf, Abetz, & Ware, 1996). Disease-specific measures include the Paediatric Asthma Quality of Life Questionnaire (PAQLQ; Juniper, Guyatt, Feeny, Ferrie, Griffith, & Townsend, 1996), the Cystic Fibrosis Questionnaire (CFQ; Modi & Quittner, 2003), and the Quality of Life in Epilepsy Inventory-Adolescents-48 (Cramer, Westbrook, Devinsky, Perrine, Glassman, & Camfield, 1999). Finally, the Pediatric Cancer Quality of Life Inventory-32 (PCQL; Varni, Katz, Seid, Quiggins, & Friedman-Bender, 1998) and the Miami Pediatric Quality of Life Questionnaire (MPQOLQ; Armstrong et al., 1999) are quality of life instruments appropriate for use with children with cancer.

3.8   Family Variables

Family variables, including family functioning, parental adjustment, and familial resources are key components of both the transactional stress and coping model and the disability stress coping model. Kazak, Barakat, and colleagues (2001) recently developed the Psychosocial Assessment Tool (PAT), which identifies the level of risk for psychosocial distress in families of children newly diagnosed with cancer. A prospective study found the PAT is valuable in the identification of psychosocial risk factors at diagnosis and is predictive of later use of psychosocial resources (Kazak et al., 2003).

Additional family focused measures include the Impact on Family Scale (IFS; Stein & Riessman, 1980; Stein & Jessop, 2003), which is a self-report measure that assesses how current family functioning is affected by an illness, and the Parent Experience of Child Illness (PECI), which measures parent adjustment related to caring for a child with a chronic illness (Bonner, Hardy, Guill, McLaughlin, Schweitzer, & Carter, 2005). The Family Adaptability and Cohesion Evaluation Scales-III (FACES-III; Olson, 1986) and the Family Environment Scale (FES; Moos & Moos, 1991) are two common instruments designed to assess family functioning that have been used in both the family and the chronic illness literature.

3.9   Summary

While many other rating scales are available, these aforementioned rating scales are the most commonly used with this population. It is noteworthy, however, that Canning and Kelleher (1994) evaluated the performance of the Child Depression Inventory (CDI), the Pediatric Symptom Checklist (PSC), and Child Behavior Checklist (CBCL) for 112 children and adolescents with chronic medical conditions and their parents in detecting emotional or behavioral disorders, compared with the diagnoses obtained by a widely utilized intensive structured psychiatric interview (Diagnostic Interview Schedule for Children, Version 2.1). The CDI, PSC, and CBCL all demonstrated low sensitivity, positive predictive value, and negative predictive value, but high specificity. The investigators concluded that the CDI, PSC, and CBCL should not be relied on as a measure of screening for psychopathology in children and adolescents with chronic medical conditions.

In a similar study, Harris et al. (1996) evaluated the Personal Adjustment and Role Skills Scale (PARS III), Child Behavior Checklist (CBCL), and Columbia Impairment Scale (CIS) in chronically ill children. The PARS III and the CBCL appear to measure similar constructs, but are likely to under identify medically ill children with comorbid psychiatric problems. Alternatively, Harris et al. suggest that the CIS, which considers more global functioning across domains, may be useful when assessing children with chronic conditions. Perrin, Stein, and Drotar (1991) also have expressed concern about the use of the CBCL for children with a chronic illness due to possible inappropriate elevations on the somatic complaints subscale. Given the inherent limitations in some rating scales, it is important to supplement data from rating scales with other assessment techniques, including interviews, observations, and other self-report measures (Kupst, 1999).

Table 5
Common Measures of Child Functioning in Pediatric Psychology

Assessment Domain	Instrument	Reference
Behavior	Conner's Parent and Teacher Rating Scales	Conners, 1997
	Child Behavior Checklist	Achenbach, 1991
	Behavior Assessment Rating Scale	Reynolds & Kamphaus, 1992
	Child Assessment Schedule	Hodges, et al., 1982
	Diagnostic Interview Schedule for Children	Shaffer, et al., 2000
	Semistructured Clinical Interview for Children and Adolescents	McConaughy & Achenbach, 1994
	Pediatric Symptom Checklist	Jellinek et al., 1999

Table 5 (continued)

Cognition	Wechsler Preschool and Primary Scale of Intelligence – Third Edition	Wechsler, 2002
	Wechsler Intelligence Scale for Children – Fourth Edition	Wechsler, 2003
	Stanford-Binet Intelligence Scale – Fifth Edition	Roid, 2003
	Wide Range Achievement Test – Third Edition	Stone et al., 1995
	Wechsler Individual Achievement Test – Second Edition	The Psychological Corporation, 2001
	Woodcock-Johnson Tests of Academic Achievement – Third Edition	Woodcock et al., 2001
	The Illness Attitude Scale	Eminson et al., 1996
	Children's Health Locus of Control Scale	Parcel & Meyer, 1978
	Children's Attributional Style Questionnaire	Kaslow et al., 1978
Affect	Children's Depression Inventory	Kovacs, 1992
	Beck Depression Inventory for Youth	Beck et al., 2001
	Revised Children's Manifest Anxiety Scale	Reynolds & Richmond, 1978
	State-Trait Anxiety Inventory for Children	Spielberger et al., 1973
	The Personal Adjustment and Roles Skills Scale	Stein & Jessop, 1990
Adherence	Self-Care Inventory	La Greca et al., 1990
	Treatment Adherence Questionnaire-CF	DiGirolamo et al., 1997
Stress and coping	UCLA Life Stress Interview for Children: Chronic Stress and Episodic Life Events	Hammen & Rudolph, 1999
	Kidcope	Spirito et al., 1988
	Children's Coping Strategies Checklist	Sandler et al., 1994
	Coping Strategies Inventory	Tobin et al., 1989
	Ways of Coping Questionnaire	Folkman & Lazarus, 1988
Quality of life	Quality of Well-Being Scale	Kaplan et al., 1989
	Child Health Questionnaire	Landgraf et al., 1996
	Paediatric Asthma Quality of Life Questionnaire	Juniper et al., 1996
	Cystic Fibrosis Questionnaire	Modi & Quittner, 2003
	Quality of Life in Epilepsy Inventory – Adolescents-48	Cramer et al., 1999

Table 5 (continued)

	Pediatric Cancer Quality of Life Inventory-32	Varni et al., 1998
	Miami Pediatric Quality of Life Questionnaire	Armstrong et al., 1999
Family variables	Psychosocial Assessment Tool (PAT)	Kazak, Barakat et al., 2001
	Impact on Family Scale	Stein & Riessman, 1980
	Parent Experience of Child Illness (PECI)	Bonner et al., 2005
	Family Adaptability and Cohesion Evaluation Scales-III	Olson, 1986
	Family Environment Scale	Moos & Moos, 1991

Treatment

Treatment methods include behavioral, cognitive-behavioral, family-based therapies, self-regulatory skills training, psychoeducational interventions, psychopharmacological interventions, and combined treatment approaches

It is widely recognized that children and adolescents with chronic illnesses are affected by both psychological and social factors as well as physical factors (Beale, 2006). Therefore, because of the heterogeneity of symptoms and needs among children with a chronic illness, different treatment plans are often needed for different patients. Treatment methods may include behavioral, cognitive-behavioral, and family-based therapies, self-regulatory skills training, psychoeducational interventions, psychopharmacological interventions, and a combination of two or more of these intervention approaches.

Prior to initiating any treatment, it is imperative that the astute clinician evaluate a child or adolescent's emotions and behavior in the context of his or her developmental level, because some behaviors and emotions will be typical or abnormal, solely depending on the age of the individual. For these reasons, Rutter (1988) described a developmental perspective as a consideration of age with respect to the prevalence, onset, remission, developmental appropriateness, and continuity or discontinuity of a disorder across the lifespan. Age of onset is a particularly important consideration for clinicians as the onset of chronic illness during adolescence is likely to have different implications for development as compared with earlier onset (Spirito, DeLawyer, & Stark, 1991). We now turn our attention to the various therapies available for children with chronic illness.

Developmental considerations should always be an important part of treatment

4.1 Methods of Treatment

4.1.1 Behavior Therapy

Behavior therapies seek to change problematic behaviors

Traditional behavior therapies are goal-oriented and focus on changing specific observable behaviors that are deemed to be problematic in one or more settings. The problem behavior is regarded as one that has been learned, not a way of thinking, and hence a behavior that can be unlearned or otherwise modified. Clinicians using behavioral treatments conduct assessments that focus on the functional analysis of a client's behavior and the resulting behavioral formulation (e.g., assessment of antecedents, behaviors, and resulting consequences). Parent training in the use of behavioral management is usually an important component of treatment.

Commonly, classical conditioning and operant techniques are used for changing maladaptive behaviors. Examples of operant techniques include positive and negative reinforcement, punishment, response cost, and extinction. Positive reinforcement encourages certain behaviors to reoccur by means of a system of tangible rewards (e.g., praise, hospital privileges, food, or points that can be exchanged for preferred activities). Rewards are provided when the child engages in the desired behavior. For example, token economies reward a child with tokens for appropriate behavior, and a token is given each time he or she behaves in an approved manner. When the child has collected sufficient tokens, he or she may redeem the tokens for some kind of prize or reward. The goal of this technique is to modify behaviors by using a secondary reinforcer (the tokens).

Negative reinforcement uses a negative, rather than a positive, reinforcer. With negative reinforcement, a behavior increases as the result of the withdrawal or termination of a stimulus (reinforcer). Punishment, in contrast, is the application of an aversive or unpleasant stimulus in response to an inappropriate or undesirable behavior. Positive punishment occurs when the application of a stimulus following a response decreases that response. Because verbal reprimands are used to reduce inappropriate behaviors and involve the application of a stimulus (reprimand) following the behavior, verbal reprimands are simply an example of positive punishment. In contrast, negative punishment occurs when a stimulus is removed following a behavior and, as a result, the behavior decreases.

Response cost is an application of a negative punishment and involves removing a specific reinforcer each time a child engages in a specific and undesired behavior. An example of response cost occurs when a child loses free-time privileges for not completing his or her homework. Extinction is the withholding of reinforcement from a previously reinforced behavior in order to decrease or eliminate that behavior. In clinical practice, positive reinforcement far exceeds the application of negative reinforcement procedures. When a behavior is only occasionally rewarded, this practice is referred to as partial or intermittent reinforcement (that is, rewards are presented on a random or unpredictable basis).

Additional behavioral techniques include systematic desensitization, relaxation training, and contingency management. Systematic desensitization, which is based on classical conditioning, has proven to be an effective treatment for children and adolescents with chronic illnesses for the purpose of reducing fear associated with painful medical interventions (e.g., lumbar punctures, blood draws) and nonpainful diagnostic studies (e.g., MRI, CT) (Harbeck-Weber, Fisher, Dittner, 2003). Systematic desensitization involves pairing relaxation with hierarchically arranged anxiety-evoking events or images (e.g., needlesticks). This technique uses gradual exposure to anxiety-producing situations to extinguish the fear response. The four stages associated with the systematic desensitization process are: relaxation training, constructing the anxiety hierarchy, desensitization in imagination, and in vivo desensitization.

Relaxation training focuses on assisting the child to engage in deep muscle relaxation. The most common form of relaxation training, progressive muscle relaxation, engages the child in focused and systematic attention, tensing and relaxing of all the body's major muscle groups. For example, a child will be instructed to tense and then relax muscles from the feet to the head, and then back to the feet, all the while focusing on the feelings of relaxing muscle groups. Muscle relaxation and deep breathing techniques can be beneficial for some children and adolescents in reducing anxiety and promoting a sense of well-being. The central activity involved in "constructing the anxiety hierarchy" is for the clinician and patient to determine the events related to the target behaviors that are ordered based on the amount of anxiety that the event evokes. The hierarchy is ranked from most to least anxiety-provoking. Desensitization in imagination involves teaching the patient to relax and then exposing him or her, in imagination, to the mildest or least anxiety-provoking stimuli first; as treatment progresses the patient is exposed progressively to stronger anxiety-provoking stimuli until the patient can tolerate extreme stimuli. Following the patient's desensitization to approximately 75–85% of the anxiety hierarchy items, in vivo desensitization is used to assist the patient in confronting anxiety-arousing stimuli in real situations.

4.1.2 Cognitive-Behavior Therapy

Cognitive-behavior therapies (CBT) are evidence-based techniques that are widely used when working with older children and adolescents. CBT is often prescribed to help children and adolescents with chronic illnesses cope with their illness and develop behaviors and strategies that help alleviate symptoms. CBT involves elements of behavior therapy and cognitive therapy. In fact, cognition and behavior are not viewed as dichotomous; instead, they are reciprocally determined, with cognition affecting behavior and vice versa (Weist & Danforth, 1998). More specifically, maladaptive behaviors are viewed as a complex interaction of cognitive factors including information processing style, problem solving and thought content, overt behaviors, and environmental experiences (Braswell & Kendall, 1988). Cognitive-behavioral approaches attempt to modify these maladaptive behaviors by applying systematic and measurable implementation of strategies designed to alter them.

One of the hallmarks of CBT is the reliance on an empirical approach that involves collecting objective and reliable information from multiple sources including the child and his or her parents, teachers, and health care providers (e.g., nurses and doctors). Interventions focus on empirically valid treatment targets. Once an intervention has begun, ongoing evaluation of the impact of treatment is considered necessary to determine whether the intervention is achieving the intended effect.

During the provision of CBT, the therapist works with the child or adolescent to identify those thoughts that are causing distress, and uses behavior therapy techniques to modify these cognitions. The following assumptions and principles are found with all cognitive-behavioral therapies (Ingram & Scott, 1990):

1. People respond to cognitive representations of events rather than to events themselves.
2. Learning is cognitively mediated.
3. Cognition mediates emotional and behavioral dysfunction.
4. At least some types of cognition can be monitored and altered.
5. Dysfunctional emotions and behaviors change when cognitions are modified.
6. Behavioral and cognitive techniques are both useful and can be integrated.

CBT is an active treatment based on changing thought patterns that lead to irrational behavior. In contrast to traditional psychoanalytic and psychodynamic therapies, CBT does not involve looking backward at root causes of psychological problems such as poor parenting and traumatic events that may be associated with abnormal behavior.

CBT interventions for children and adolescents with chronic illnesses consider the dynamic and often complex interactions among behavior, cognition, affect, social factors, and environmental conditions. CBT clinicians may simultaneously or sequentially serve in the role of a diagnostician, consultant, or educator, and often function as a "coach" providing short-term treatment to the child and/or family (Kendall, 2000). The clinician is expected to educate the child and family about the disorder (e.g., depression), the cognitive model, and the therapy process, as well as provide training in the needed skill areas for the young client and/or parents (Braswell & Kendall, 2001).

> **Cognitive-behavior therapy seeks to change thought patterns that lead to maladaptive behavior**

CBT with children and adolescents differs in important ways in comparison to treatment with adults (Braswell & Kendall, 2001). These differences include: (a) the need for careful attention to a young client's level of cognitive and affective development; (b) use of developmentally-appropriate modes of delivery of the therapy content; (c) the recognition of the differences in how young clients come to treatment versus adults who are often self-referred; and (d) recognition of the extent to which a young client is embedded in his or her social context.

CBT with children uses various forms of enactive, performance-based procedures as well as cognitive interventions to produce changes in thinking, feeling, and behavior (Kendall, 2000). Cognitive-behavioral skills aim to promote relaxation and self-mastery. Behavioral procedures include, but are not limited to, modeling, role-playing, guided imagery, positive self-talk, conscious breathing, refocusing, and biofeedback. Modeling helps children learn by observing others to achieve the elimination of behavioral deficits. Role-playing exercises provide the child or adolescent with performance-based learning experiences. Guided imagery entails replacing fearful thoughts with visualizations of peaceful, pleasant, and nurturing scenes. The main goal of positive self-talk is learning to replace negative, fearful thoughts with reassuring, positive messages. Refocusing involves the conscious redirection of the child's attention from stressful stimuli to relaxing or entertaining stimuli. Conscious breathing entails the focused attention of breathing to enhance relaxation. Another useful behavioral technique is deep breathing, which entails training the child to inhale purposefully and slowly, expanding the diaphragm, and then purposefully exhaling. Finally, biofeedback promotes conscious relaxation via feedback provided by means of physiological monitoring equipment.

Additional components of CBT may include the use of tasks and homework assigned by the therapist, cognitive restructuring, self-regulation, affective education, and behavioral contingencies. Cognitive restructuring methods focus on addressing the child or adolescent's negative cognitive representations. Initially, the therapist assists the client in becoming aware of self-statements, expectancies, assumptions, or beliefs that reflect maladaptive ways of thinking about oneself, the world, and/or the future. Subsequently, the therapist and client examine any possible connections between the negative thoughts and the client's emotional experience. Finally, the therapist and client work together to identify, create, and test more adaptive ways of thinking (Braswell & Kendall, 2001). Self-regulation approaches aim to provide young people with carefully planned experiences that help them develop more adaptive problem-solving strategies. The main goal of affective education is to assist the child or adolescent learn why we have emotions, their use and misuse, and the identification of different levels of expression. Finally, behavioral contingency approaches involve the use of reward systems and punishment (e.g., time outs).

4.1.3   Behavioral and Cognitive-Behavioral Interventions – Empirical Support and Clinical Trials

In this section we review selected research, particularly intervention trials, in the context of behavioral and/or cognitive-behavioral therapies when working with children and adolescents with chronic illness (i.e., asthma, cancer, cystic fibrosis, diabetes mellitus, sickle cell disease). Our review will focus on the results and clinical implications of these interventions as they relate to overall psychological adjustment (e.g., depression, anxiety, disruptive behavior), psychosocial factors (e.g., self-efficacy, quality of life, family functioning), coping and pain management, and adherence to medical treatment for children and adolescents with a chronic illness.

4.1.4   Psychological Adjustment

Asthma

There is compelling evidence to support the contention that children and adolescents with asthma are at particular risk for problems in psychological adjustment and adaptation with their disease. For example, a meta-analytic review of the behavioral adjustment of children and adolescents with asthma revealed that they have more behavioral difficulties than do their healthy peers, and the effect size for internalizing behaviors (e.g., anxiety, depression) was greater than that for externalizing behaviors (McQuaid et al., 2001). Despite these important findings, few studies have specifically focused on improving the psychological adaptation of children with asthma as the primary goal of the study (Drotar, 2006).

In one of the few behavioral intervention studies that specifically targeted the psychological and behavioral adjustment of children with asthma, Perrin, MacLean, Gortmaker, and Asher (1992) conducted a randomized controlled trial that investigated the efficacy of combined education, stress management, and contingency coping exercises. Stress management techniques used relaxation training in which children were taught to engage in deep breathing exercises through guided imagery and muscle relaxation. Contingency coping exercises focused on enhancing children's ability to cope with the challenges associated with the management of asthma symptoms. The Child Behavior Checklist (CBCL) was used to assess psychological functioning before and after the intervention. Children in the intervention group demonstrated fewer behavioral adjustment problems and less frequent internalizing symptoms compared to the no treatment control group.

Given that asthma is the leading cause of chronic illness among children and adolescents in the United States, it is likely that mental health practitioners will encounter children with asthma in their practice. McQuaid and Walders (2003) proposed several roles for mental health practitioners in their treatment and management of children and adolescents with asthma, including: (a) providing asthma education to the patient and family; (b) identification and treatment of psychosocial barriers to effective asthma management; and (c) employing effective psychosocial intervention techniques to enhance family-based management behaviors.

Cancer

The majority of psychological intervention approaches designed to reduce the psychological distress experienced by some children with cancer have focused on the promotion of social skills, school reintegration, and psychological adaptation of survivors and parents (Drotar, 2006). For example, Varni, Katz, Colegrove, and Dolgin (1993) conducted a randomized controlled trial that evaluated a social skills intervention for children and adolescents with newly diagnosed cancer as compared to a standard school reintegration group. Children and adolescents who were randomized to the social skills group participated in individual therapy sessions dedicated to provide instruction in problem-solving, assertiveness training, and ways to appropriately handle teasing from peers. The problem-solving intervention focused on teaching children how to appropriately handle cancer-related interpersonal difficulties with regard to peers, teachers, parents, and siblings. The goal of assertiveness training was to improve children's ability to effectively express their thoughts, wishes, and concerns to others. Finally, children were taught to cope with verbal and physical teasing associated with changes in their physical appearance (e.g., hair loss, weight gain or loss, surgical disfigurement). Assessment included measures of child depression, anxiety, self-esteem, perceived social support, parent-reported behavioral and emotional problems, and social competence. Although both groups demonstrated reduced anxiety and behavioral problems and increased social support following the intervention, children in the social skills group reported fewer behavioral problems and reduced state anxiety, compared to the standard school reintegration group.

Cystic Fibrosis

Thompson and colleagues (1992; 1998) reported that school-age children with cystic fibrosis (CF) may be at risk for problems related to anxiety and externalizing behavior, and recommend that psychological interventions focus on ameliorating these difficulties. Unfortunately, few controlled trials have investigated the enhancement of psychological adjustment among children and adolescents with CF (Drotar, 2006). For example, Glasscoe and Quittner (2003) recently conducted a meta-analysis that examined psychological interventions for CF. These reviewers were unable to locate any interventions related to cognitive-behavior therapy, family therapy, or other psychotherapies that focus on assisting individuals with CF adjust and adapt to the emotional difficulties associated with this disease.

Hains, Davies, Behrens, and Biller (1997) examined the effectiveness of a cognitive-behavioral intervention that included training in cognitive restructuring and problem-solving for the purpose of enhancing the ability of adolescents with CF to cope with daily stressors. Outcome measures included coping, trait anxiety, perceptions of functional disability, and parental reports of behavior. Participants reported decreased anxiety, decreased maladaptive coping with CF-related problems, decreased functional disability, and increased positive coping with CF-related problems.

Diabetes Mellitus

There is some evidence to suggest that children and adolescents with type I insulin-dependent diabetes mellitus are at increased risk for emotional and behavioral problems such as depression, anxiety, and eating disorders (Drotar, 2006). Wysocki et al. (2003) suggest the use of cognitive-behavioral treatments that incorporate stress management techniques, problem solving, and conflict resolution skills may improve the psychological adjustment of children and adolescents with diabetes. A recent meta-analysis of randomized controlled trials of psychological interventions in patients with type I diabetes found positive effects for psychological intervention on psychological distress for children and adolescents (Winkley, Ismail, Eisler, & Landau, 2006).

Sickle Cell Disease

Children and adolescents with sickle-cell disease (SCD) are at particular risk for the development of psychiatric disorders, especially internalizing behavior problems such as depression and anxiety. Sickle cell disease is a life-long disorder that is characterized by ongoing pain and requires consistent medical attention. Gil, Anthony, Carson, Redding-Lallinger, Daeschner, and Ware (2001) conducted a randomized controlled trial that evaluated a behavioral intervention for children and adolescents with SCD. Behavioral techniques included deep breathing, relaxation, pleasant imagery, and calming self-statements. Participants in the intervention group endorsed a reduction of negative thinking and lower levels of pain at two- to three-weeks follow-up and increased coping attempts at one-month follow-up. However, no differences were found between the intervention and standard care group on illness-coping strategies or on assessments of anxiety and depression. Unfortunately, there are few intervention studies for children and adolescents with SCD that focus on reducing problems in adjustment (Lemanek et al., 2003).

Summary

Children and adolescents with a chronic illness may be at higher risk for specific psychological or psychosocial adjustment difficulties relative to healthy peers. Therefore, mental health providers should assist in building effective coping skills, particularly given their increased risk of the development of symptoms of anxiety, depression, grief, anger, and/or guilt that often accompany chronic illness. Interventions that provide positive reinforcement for healthy behaviors and extinguish reinforcement for pain behaviors can enhance the coping behaviors of children with chronic illness.

4.1.5 Psychosocial Factors, Coping, and Pain Management

Asthma

Asthma is a complex disease that involves psychosocial factors such as self-efficacy, self-worth and social competence, locus of control, attributions, family functioning, and social support variables. As one example, psychosocial stress of a family unit may impede the family's ability to adhere to treatment recommendations. Therefore, it is important that psychosocial interventions address stress, coping, and problem solving among children and families living with asthma.

Psychosocial interventions for asthma should address stress, coping, and problem solving

Walders, Kercsmar, Schluchter, Redline, Kirchner, and Drotar (2006) conducted a randomized-controlled clinical trial that evaluated the effectiveness of an interdisciplinary intervention for pediatric asthma. The interdisciplinary intervention group received medical care, asthma education, and brief problem-solving therapy, whereas the control group received medical care alone. Both groups demonstrated significant reductions in asthma symptoms and reported improvements in quality of life without any between-group differences identified over the course of follow-up. However, the intervention group demonstrated less frequent health-care utilization than the comparison group at 12-month follow-up. Specifically, only 28% of children in the interdisciplinary intervention required emergency department or inpatient services for asthma, compared with 41% of those receiving standard care.

Castes, Hagel, Palenque, Canelones, Corao, and Lynch (1999) conducted a prospective study that evaluated the effectiveness of psychosocial intervention on the immunological status and clinical management of children with asthma. Both groups received conventional asthma management. However, children in the experimental group received a 6-month psychosocial intervention consisting of relaxation, guided imagery, and self-esteem workshops. The number of asthma attacks and use of bronchodilator medication were significantly reduced for participants in the experimental group, and pulmonary function improved significantly when compared to controls. In addition, participants in the experimental group demonstrated a reduction in the immunoglobulin E (IgE) responses to the most prevalent allergen, *Ascaris lumbricoides*.

Cancer

Children and adolescents may encounter psychological distress as well as physiological pain during and after their cancer treatment. These youths may experience pain from metastatic disease, procedural-related pain (e.g., venipuncture, lumbar punctures, bone marrow aspirations), and/or pain from various therapies (e.g., chemotherapy, radiation), which may significantly affect their quality of life. Children and adolescents often become frustrated with the physiological pain and restriction of activities due to cancer treatment and consequently become depressed and angry. Therefore, particularly salient psychosocial interventions for children and adolescents with cancer, as well as childhood survivors of cancer, include behavioral, cognitive, and combined cognitive-behavioral approaches that target psychosocial factors and coping and pain management.

Although the rate of posttraumatic stress disorder (PTSD) in childhood cancer survivors is low (5%–10%) (Erickson & Steiner, 2001; Kazak, Prusak et al., 2001), the rate is considerably higher when assessing symptom clusters (e.g., reexperiencing, arousal; Brown, Madan-Swain, & Lambert, 2003; Erickson & Steiner, 2001; Kazak, Prusak et al., 2001). Additional reports suggest high rates of posttraumatic stress disorder (PTSD) and posttraumatic stress symptoms (PTSS) for survivors of childhood cancer when they are young adults (15%–21%; Hobbie et al., 2000; Rourke, Hobbie, & Kazak, 2002).

Kazak, Alderfer, Streisand, and colleagues (2004) conducted a cognitive-behavioral and family therapy manualized intervention for adolescent survivors of childhood cancer and their families. This wait-list control, randomized clinical trial used the Surviving Cancer Competently Intervention Program that integrates cognitive behavioral and family therapeutic approaches. Survivors and family members identify ongoing distressing beliefs about cancer, receive training in cognitive-behavioral approaches (e.g., self-talk and reframing) for enhancing coping skills. They also are exposed to an interpersonal systems framework that assists in the identification of the current and likely future impact of cancer on the family. Decreased symptoms of arousal in adolescent survivors of cancer in the intervention group were found postintervention, relative to the wait-list control group.

Interventions also are needed for survivors of cancer that focus on the psychological symptoms associated with surviving cancer such as tension, depression, or anxiety, as well as social aspects such as impaired peer relations. Schwartz, Feinberg, Jilinskala, and Applegate (1999) conducted a psychosocial intervention for adolescent and young adult cancer survivors that included components of support, education, and recreation. Dependent measures included health-related quality of life and psychological well-being. Increased quality of life was found for those in the intervention group relative to the healthy controls. In addition, ratings of perceived improved quality of life persisted at 3-month follow-up.

Pain management is often a primary concern for a child or adolescent with cancer. In fact, pain typically represents one of the child or adolescent's greatest fears. Mental health providers should devise treatment plans that ease or even eliminate pain during the treatment process. Powers (1999) reviewed empirically supported treatments of procedure-related pain and observed that behavioral pain management and relaxation techniques qualify as empirically validated treatments for reduction of anxiety and joint pain during intensive medical procedures. Additional cognitive-behavioral approaches for the management of pain include imagery, hypnosis, modeling, and positive reinforcement. Relaxation and distraction also have demonstrated positive effects for reducing the adverse side effects associated with chemotherapy and associated nausea (for a review, see McQuaid & Nassau, 1999). In general, interventions that provide educational information, modeling, and behavioral reversal are used prior to the commencement of the painful procedure. Interventions used during the procedure may include hypnosis, imagery distraction, controlled breathing, and progressive muscle relaxation. Finally, positive reinforcement or rewards for adaptive coping are provided following the procedure.

Relaxation for pain management involves guiding the child through relaxation exercises such as deep breathing and stretching to reduce discomfort. School-age children and older adolescents may find watching TV or listening to music to be a viable and helpful distraction. The goal of imagery as an intervention is to assist the child or adolescent by guiding them through an imaginary mental image of sights, sounds, tastes, smells, and feelings that can often help shift attention away from the pain. Professionals who use hypnosis guide children into an altered state of consciousness that helps them concentrate on images or sensations other than their pain. Richardson, Smith, McCall, and Pilkington (2006) recently reviewed studies that used hypnosis interventions for procedure-related pain and distress in pediatric cancer patients. They concluded that hypnosis for pediatric cancer patients has potential as a clinically valuable intervention for procedure-related pain and distress.

Relaxation exercises are an important component of pain management

Cystic Fibrosis

Cystic fibrosis (CF) dramatically influences psychosocial functioning. Children and adolescents with CF must often negotiate multiple disease-related stressors that include complex regimen adherence, frequent coughing attacks, and missing school due to pulmonary complications (Hains et al., 1997). Children and adolescents with poor coping skills are likely to struggle with these stressors.

Hains and colleagues (1997) used cognitive-behavioral interventions that specifically focus on coping behaviors for youth with cystic fibrosis. The intervention included a cognitive restructuring phase in which participants ($N = 5$) were taught to challenge and restructure negative cognitions about stressful events. Problem-solving training focused on defining the problem, considering solutions to solve the problem, generating consequences, and making a decision based on this process. Outcome measures included trait anxiety, coping, functional disability, and parental reports of psychological adaptation. Significant decreases in anxiety, maladaptive coping with CF-related problems, and functional disability were found, as well as increases in positive coping with CF-related problems. In a follow-up study with a small sample of young adults with CF ($N = 4$) using the above intervention, Hains, Davies, Behrens, Freeman, and Biller (2001) found decreased anxiety ($n = 1$), anger ($n = 1$), functional disability ($n = 2$), as well as increases in approach and avoidant coping ($n = 2$).

Diabetes Mellitus

Psychosocial factors, such as stress management and coping skills, play a crucial role in the management of children with type I insulin-dependent diabetes mellitus. Specifically, there is evidence to indicate that psychosocial factors impair blood glucose control and increase the frequency of long-term complications associated with this life-long disease (Kaplan, Saddock, & Grebb, 1994). Diabetes management is complex and often requires children or adolescents to take responsibility for managing their health with daily injections, careful monitoring of diet, exercise, and blood glucose levels for the rest of their lives. Consequently, children and adolescents with diabetes often experience significant levels of stress related to managing and coping with their illness and the demands of daily life.

The effectiveness of stress management training programs in helping children and adolescents with diabetes cope with stress has been carefully examined. Similar to their studies with children with cystic fibrosis, Hains and colleagues (2001) used both cognitive-restructuring and problem-solv-

Stress management exercises may prove useful for children with diabetes

ing strategies as part of a cognitive-behavioral intervention for adolescents with metabolic control problems. During the cognitive restructuring phases, participants were taught to challenge and restructure negative cognitions about both diabetes and nondiabetes-related stressful events. Problem-solving training focused on defining the problem, considering solutions to solve the problem, generating consequences, and making a decision based on this process. Assessment measures included perceived use of coping strategies, anxiety level, disease-specific stress, and indices of glycemic control. The training group improved from pretest to posttest and from pretest to follow-up on anxiety, coping, and stress measures. In contrast, no differences were found in the control group.

Cook, Herold, Edidin, and Briars (2002) conducted a randomized controlled trial that evaluated the effectiveness of diabetes-related problem-solving training for adolescents with type I diabetes. The intervention group demonstrated improved problem-solving skills compared to the standard care group, although no between-group differences were maintained at six-month follow-up. Finally, Grey, Boland, Davidson, Li, and Tamborlane (2000) conducted a self-management program for teens with type I diabetes; This intervention involved enhancing coping and social problem solving, teaching social skills, cognitive behavior modification, and conflict resolution. Improvements in both metabolic control and quality of life were found, and, in addition, the program enhanced teens' effectiveness in other areas of their lives.

Sickle Cell Disease

Pain is one of the primary symptoms of sickle cell disease (SCD) in both children and adolescents. The physical and psychological consequences of acute severe pain and chronic pain in sickle cell disease often interferes with typical childhood functioning. For example, impairments in academic achievement, sleep, and social activities are commonly associated with the acute and recurrent pain crises experienced by children and adolescents with SCD (Gil, porter, Ready, Workman, Sedway, & Anthony, 2000).

> Cognitive-behavioral techniques include instruction of psychological coping skills for pain management for children with sickle cell disease

For this reason, cognitive-behavioral techniques, interventions aimed at behavioral change, and social support interventions have focused on improving pain management in children and adolescents with SCD. A common theme shared among these interventions is the instruction of psychological coping skills for pain management. Gil and colleagues (1997) conducted a randomized controlled clinical trial that evaluated a cognitive-behavioral coping intervention for children and adolescents with SCD. Cognitive-behavioral techniques included deep breathing, relaxation, pleasant imagery, and calming self-statements. In this trial, therapists provided a definition and explanation of how cognitive coping strategies could be employed to reduce pain. Subsequently, therapists described, modeled, and practiced each stage of the treatment with the participant. Finally, therapists telephoned the children once a week to remind them to practice their newly learned strategies. Intervention sessions included one treatment session (45 minutes) and one brief follow-up session. Children in the intervention group reported decreased negative thinking and were less likely to report pain (when exposed to a laboratory pain stimulus), compared with their peers in a control group that received standard medical care. However, reports of active coping did not differ between the intervention and control group.

In another controlled trial of a cognitive-behavioral intervention to manage pain for children and adolescents with SCD, 65 children and 32 adolescents with SCD were randomly assigned to a relaxation, art therapy, or an attention-control group (Broome, Maikler, Kelber, Bailey, & Lea, 2001). The children and adolescents in the relaxation group had fewer emergency room and clinic visits, and they increased their use of prevention strategies. For adolescents, there also was an increase in active coping strategies from preintervention to one-year follow-up. Finally, a review of empirically supported psychosocial interventions for pain concluded that cognitive-behavioral techniques, as a type of intervention for treating sickle cell pain, are probably efficacious interventions (Chen, Cole, & Kato, 2004). Additional alternative therapies such as acupuncture, massage, or biofeedback may assist in reducing discomfort due to pain.

Summary

Psychosocial factors, coping, and pain management play a significant role in the evaluation and treatment of children and adolescents with chronic illness and their families. Practitioners should be aware of coping styles, not only in the child, but among family members as well, particularly since parental coping style may directly affect the child's approach to coping. Due to the variability associated with illness type, interventions focusing on pain management should target relevant indices of pain in each chronic illness. For example, pain management interventions for children with sickle cell disease would likely address pain crises while interventions for cancer may focus on easing the pain associated with various procedures such as lumbar punctures.

4.1.6   Adherence

Asthma

Medical management of pediatric asthma may include use of inhaled corticosteroids, rescue inhalers, nebulized medications, and allergy medications. In addition, the environment including second hand smoke and dust may also contribute to symptoms. Thus, treatment of the disease often involves control of the environment, including using high efficiency particulate air (HEPA) filters and avoiding second hand smoke. Effective management requires active engagement of patients and their families in managing their own living conditions. However, given the complexity of the treatment regimen for asthma, children and adolescents may become confused when faced with multiple inhalers and lose motivation if they do not see rapid improvements in their symptoms, resulting in under use of asthma medication. Children's adherence in one study was less than half of prescribed doses (48%), with older children exhibiting less adherence to prescribed medication than younger children (McQuaid, Kopel, Klein, & Fritz, 2003). The most frequently identified barriers to treatment adherence for both asthma and cystic fibrosis include forgetting, oppositional behaviors, and difficulties with time management (Modi &

Quittner, 2006). A qualitative study on children's adherence to asthma medications found similar results; in this study the most frequent barriers to medication adherence were lack of motivation, difficulties remembering, and social barriers (Penza-Clyve, Mansell, & McQuaid, 2004).

Behavioral strategies are often used in adherence-related interventions

A review of empirical studies of psychological interventions for nonadherence to medical regimens for pediatric chronic illnesses, including asthma, found that behavioral strategies were frequently incorporated into adherence-related interventions (Lemanek, Kamps, & Chung, 2001). Components of these strategies include self-regulatory procedures, such as self-monitoring of pulmonary functioning and asthma management, or reinforcement-based procedures, such as contracting and token systems. The authors conclude that behavioral strategies appear promising for promoting adherence to asthma regimens.

Bartlett, Lukk, Butz, Lampros-Klein, and Rand (2002) conducted a pilot study among inner-city children with asthma that examined the effectiveness of an intervention for enhancing adherence to the daily use of inhaled steroids. The program included well established social learning strategies such as goal-setting, monitoring, feedback, reinforcement, and enhanced self-efficacy. Specifically, the intervention targeted known barriers to medication use, taught problem-solving strategies and opportunities, promoted self-efficacy in children and parents for medication adherence, and provided constant feedback about treatment goals. The rate of underutilization of medication decreased from 51.2% to 25.4%, while the appropriate use of medication improved from 28.6% at baseline to 51.4% at the end of the four-week intervention.

Cancer

Nonadherence also poses a significant threat to the successful treatment of pediatric cancer, especially among adolescents (Beale, Bradlyn, & Kato, 2003). Although a complete understanding of the extent of nonadherence among children with cancer is unknown, a substantial proportion of children are minimally adherent, with nonadherence rates highest in adolescents (Partridge, Avorn, Wang, & Winer, 2002). For example, one study reported rates of nonadherence above 50% for adolescents following oral medication regimes (Festa, Tamaroff, Chasalow, & Lanzkowsky, 1992). Despite the clear importance of adherence to pediatric cancer treatments, no adherence-related intervention studies in children with cancer have been reported in the peer-reviewed literature (Drotar, 2006).

Cystic Fibrosis

Medical management of the treatment regimen for cystic fibrosis (CF) may include taking enzymes, airway clearance, nutrition, and nebulized medications. Modi and Quittner (2006) examined parent and child reports of barriers to treatment adherence for CF and found that 50% of children with CF endorsed barriers for enzymes, 75% for airway clearance, 44% for nutrition, and 75% for nebulized medications (e.g., dornase alpha, inhaled tobramycin, and albuterol). Of parents of children with CF, 77% endorsed barriers for enzymes, 92% for airway clearance, 69% for nutrition, and 73% for nebulized medications.

In a recent investigation using objective measures of treatment adherence for CF, rates of overall adherence were below 50% for children with CF (Modi,

Lim, Yu, Geller, Wagner, & Quittner, 2006). Specifically, rates of adherence to enzyme medications, which were measured with electronic and diary measures, ranged from 27% to 46%. The investigators conclude that participants in their study demonstrated generally poor adherence to the treatment regimen.

Glasscoe and Quittner (2003) conducted a review of the literature related to psychological interventions for CF, including behavioral interventions designed to improve dietary intake in children up to 12 years of age. There was insufficient evidence to demonstrate whether behavioral interventions improve outcomes for dietary intake. On the other hand, Stark et al. (2003) have proposed that behavioral interventions that emphasize self-monitoring, goal setting, and shaping to structure the delivery of treatment may prove beneficial for increasing energy intake and weight gain in children with cystic fibrosis.

Diabetes Mellitus

Children and adolescents with diabetes must pay careful attention to diet, insulin administration, frequent monitoring of blood glucose levels, regular exercise, and routine medical care. Given the complexity and responsibility associated with the diabetes treatment regimen, many children and adolescents find it difficult to achieve and maintain effective self-management and adherence-related behaviors. However, younger children with diabetes tend to demonstrate better adherence than their adolescent counterparts.

Winkley, Landau, Eisler, and Ismail (2006) conducted a meta-analysis of randomized controlled trials of psychological interventions to improve glycemic control in children and adolescents with type I diabetes. Findings revealed weak evidence for the effectiveness of psychological treatments in improving glycemic control in children and adolescents. In another review of empirically supported treatments for nonadherence to treatment regimens for children and adolescent with diabetes, Lemanek et al. (2001) observed that operant learning procedures are probably efficacious, and cognitive-behavioral strategies are especially promising as interventions. Finally, Wysocki (2006) reviewed behavioral intervention studies targeting treatment adherence for pediatric diabetes and concluded that behavioral contracting and behavior modification are effective techniques for improving adherence in this population.

Wysocki, Green, and Huxtable (1989), who evaluated self-monitoring of blood glucose compliance among adolescents with type I diabetes, documented the value of behavioral contracting. Assessment instruments included reflectance meters with memory to assess the target behavior. The researchers used three groups: 12 participants received standard medical care (conventional therapy group), 15 used reflective meters alone (meter alone group), and 15 used a meter and earned money contingent on meeting monthly testing goals (meter plus contract group). Adherence exceeded 80% for the meter plus contract group, whereas adherence rates between 50–60% were achieved in the meter alone group. Finally, glycemic control was higher in the meter alone and meter plus contract groups relative to the conventional therapy group.

Sickle Cell Disease

One recent study found that low family stress and the sharing of responsibilities for chelation therapy between parents and children was associated with better adherence to home deferoxamine administration (a chelating agent used to remove excess iron from the body) administration for children with sickle cell disease (SCD) (Treadwell et al., 2005). The use of behavioral contracts for children and adolescents with SCD has been recommended as an appropriate intervention to enhance treatment adherence (Collins, Kaslow, Doepke, Eckman, & Johnson, 1998). The primary goals of this intervention are to decrease the reliance on the health care system, decrease the use of medications, and reduce the number of hospitalizations. Unfortunately, cognitive-behavioral interventions have had a disappointing effect on adherence behaviors for children and adolescents with sickle cell disease (Chen et al., 2004; Drotar, 2006).

Summary

Few studies have examined treatment adherence for pediatric cancer, cystic fibrosis, and sickle cell disease

Providers working with children and adolescents with chronic illness should be aware of appropriate developmental expectations for illness management when designing and implementing interventions for adherence-related behaviors. For example, due to issues of peer conformity, it is important to know that adolescents generally achieve lower adherence rates than their younger counterparts. While the adherence-related intervention literature is fairly compelling for asthma and diabetes, there is a surprising dearth of intervention studies related to treatment adherence for pediatric cancer, cystic fibrosis, and sickle cell disease.

4.1.7   Family Systems Interventions

Chronic illness and its associated day-to-day management profoundly affect the family life of the child or adolescent. Families in turn may provide support for a child with a chronic illness and a means of coping with the hardships associated with a disease. Family functioning is an important predictor of psychological functioning of children with chronic illness (Quittner & DiGirolamo, 1998). The stress associated with parenting a child with chronic illness may affect families' organization and coping patterns.

The extant literature supports a link between family cohesion and support to disease adjustment, adaptation, and in many cases adherence with the disease regimen among children with chronic illnesses (Hanson, 1992; Holmes, Yu, & Frentz, 1999; Soliday, Kool, & Lande, 2000; Thompson et al., 1999). Children with a chronic illness generally fare better when the family is cohesive, supportive, the mother is coping well, and communication is open and clear (Wallander & Thompson, 1995). When the family is too cohesive or overly controlling, the child may encounter difficulty with adaptation to illness and disease management. Despite the compelling body of child and adolescent psychology literature attesting to the importance of the family, relatively few studies have actually tested family-system-focused interventions for children and adolescents with various chronic illnesses. We review the basic principles of family-systems therapies in relation to children with chronic illness, and describe relevant interventions with specific illness populations.

All family therapies seek to modify relationships within a family to achieve harmony and, in the case of children and adolescents with chronic illness, adaptation. The family-systems model is most often applied to families of children who have a chronic illness because it concentrates on the family's influence on individual behavior within a social context. More specifically, the model emphasizes the role of family dynamics or interactions in response to the stress associated with the child's illness (Thompson & Gustafson, 1996).

Family systems interventions differ from individual therapy in that the focus is on the emotional life of the family as a unit, rather than on the child or adolescent who may have been labeled "the patient." The three major assumptions of family therapy are that: (a) it is logical and economical to treat together all those family members who exist and operate within a system of relationships; (b) the problems of the "identified patient" are only symptoms, and the family itself is the client or unit of treatment; and (c) the task of the therapist is to modify the relationships within the family system (Sue, Sue, & Sue, 1994). In relation to chronic illness, family systems interventions may be particularly useful in chronic medical conditions (e.g., abdominal pain, headaches, asthma) that result from familial dysfunction (e.g., marital discord, alcohol and substance abuse, physical and other abuse), or where disease states are exacerbated by familial stressors. Systemic family therapies for children and adolescents with chronic illness include multi-systemic family therapy (MST), behavioral family systems therapy (BFST), and structural family therapy (SFT).

Multisystemic family therapy addresses the family as a system, using a multidisciplinary approach within a nested ecological system (Henggeler, Schoenwald, Borduin, Rowland, & Cunningham, 1998). MST focuses on intrafamily processes such as family structure, communication, emotional cohesion, and problem-solving style. MST is based on systems theory and social ecology theory. It draws from multiple human services approaches, and attempts to establish "ecological validity" in developing a fit between interventions and problems as identified and understood in terms of multiple levels of family functioning. One of the main benefits of MST, compared to other family therapy interventions, is that this approach encompasses the individual adolescent, the family system, and the broader community systems within which the family operates (i.e., school, hospital) (Ellis, Naar-King, Frey, Rowland, & Greger, 2003).

Principles associated with MST include: (a) the use of assessment to understand the fit between problems and the broader system context; (b) an emphasis on the positive and the building of systemic strengths for change; (c) the promotion of responsible behaviors and the lessening of irresponsible behavior; (d) a focus on interventions that are present focused, action-oriented, and well-defined; (e) the targeting on sequences of behaviors within and between multiple systems; (f) interventions that are developmentally appropriate to needs of youth; (g) interventions that are designed to require daily/weekly efforts by family members; (h) ongoing evaluation of intervention effectiveness from multiple perspectives; and finally, (i) interventions that are designed to promote long-term maintenance and generalization of intervention efforts and behaviors (Henggeler et al., 1998).

MST has been used primarily in the treatment of adolescents with severe antisocial behavior; However, very recent evidence indicates it may be effective when applied to adolescents with various chronic illnesses. For example, Ellis and colleagues (2003) examined the effectiveness of multisystemic

Family therapies for children and adolescents with chronic illness seek to modify relationships within a family to achieve better adaptation

therapy for improving poor metabolic control among four adolescents with insulin-dependent type I diabetes mellitus. Participants showed improvements in health status and made less use of medical services including fewer hospitalizations and emergency room visits.

In a related study, MST was compared to a control group for measuring improved regimen adherence and metabolic control among adolescents with poorly controlled type I diabetes. Adolescents who received MST had significantly improved adherence to blood glucose testing and enhanced metabolic control from study entry to the six-month posttest, whereas controls did not show these changes. Adolescents receiving MST also had fewer inpatient admissions at the six-month follow-up evaluation (Ellis, Naar-King, Frey, Templin, Rowland, & Cakan, 2005).

Similar results were found for a randomized trial of MST among adolescents with chronically poorly controlled type I diabetes; specifically, adolescents who received MST demonstrated improved frequency of blood glucose testing, enhanced metabolic control, and a decrease in health care utilization (i.e., inpatient admissions) (Ellis, Frey, Naar-King, Templin, Cunningham, & Cakan, 2005). The family intervention in this trial involved improving parental involvement, monitoring, and discipline regarding the adolescents' diabetes regimen, developing family organizational routines such as regular meal times, and teaching caregivers to communicate effectively and productively with each other about the adolescents' medical regimen (Ellis, Frey et al., 2005).

Finally, MST was recently evaluated for antiretroviral adherence and health outcomes in HIV-infected pediatric patients. General HIV knowledge on the part of caregivers improved significantly over the course of treatment, while viral loads for the adolescents were found to decrease significantly from referral to the end of MST treatment. The investigators conclude that MST holds promise as an intervention for improving health outcomes among pediatric patients with HIV (Ellis, Naar-King, Cunningham, & Secord, 2006).

Behavioral family systems therapy (BFST) has demonstrated promise as an intervention for adolescents with conduct problems (Robin & Foster, 1989), adherence to diabetes treatment (Wysocki, Greco, Harris, Bubb, & White, 2001), and adherence to treatment in adolescents with cystic fibrosis (Quittner, Drotar, Ievers-Landis, Seidner, Slocum, & Jacobsen, 2000). BFST is a form of behavioral therapy that focuses on family relationships and conflict resolution. The four components of BFST include: (a) training in problem-solving and conflict resolution; (b) family communication skills training; (c) cognitive restructuring of family members' exaggerated beliefs; and finally, (d) systemic family therapy to modify structural/functional anomalies that might impede problem-solving or communication. BFST interventions focus on reducing coercive family processes by changing the family environment so that it becomes more attuned to the developmental demands of increased independence, autonomy, and decision-making that is common in adolescence (Harris, Harris, & Mertlich, 2005).

Wysocki and colleagues (2001) compared BFST to education and support or current therapy on measures of treatment adherence, psychological adjustment to diabetes, and diabetes control at the 6- and 12-month follow-up. Participants in the BFST group evidenced better health behaviors and psychosocial outcomes than those adolescents with diabetes who participated in the educational/support group treatment arm or adolescents in the control group. In a study of treatment adherence for adolescents with cystic fibrosis, Quittner, Drotar, Ievers-Landis, and De Lambo (2004) found that BFST was effective in reducing family conflict as reported by the mothers and adolescents, enhanced communication regarding the disease, and resulted in fewer CF-specific problems. However, in a similar study using BFST with adolescents with poorly controlled diabetes, the initially positive posttreatment findings of decreased general family conflict, diabetes-related conflict, and behavior problems were no longer present at six-month follow-up (Harris et al., 2005).

Structural family therapy has also been used as an intervention for addressing behavior problems in children and adolescents. Minuchin, Montalvo, Guerney, Rosman, and Schumer (1967) developed the model of structural family therapy through their early work with a lower socioeconomic population and later expanded their program of research to psychosomatic populations. In the structural family approach, the disorder is viewed as being a result of a system of relationships that need to be strategically addressed. Problems are purported to arise because family members are either too involved (enmeshment) or too little involved with each other. In the case of children with chronic illness, this may take the form of one or both parents becoming enmeshed with their child in order to play the role of caretakers. Conversely, the stress of caring for a child with a chronic illness may instead result in disengagement by a parent.

Accordingly, therapeutic interventions target the restructuring of family interactions, often using conflict around homeostatic patterns as the stimulus for change. The focus of structural family therapy is on the family system, particularly in terms of family organization (marital, parental, and sibling subsystems), family management styles, family communication styles, family problem solving style, shared family beliefs, and emotional engagement and cohesion among family members. Techniques include challenging directly absent or rigid boundaries, unbalancing the family equilibrium by temporarily joining with one member of the family against others or setting homework tasks designed to restore hierarchies within the family (e.g., redefining parental roles). Structural family therapy has been shown to reduce conflicts, anger, negative communications, and symptoms of internalizing (e.g., anxiety, depression) and externalizing disorders (e.g., acting out) (Barkley, Guevremont, Anastopoulous, & Fletcher, 1992).

Early research demonstrated that structural family therapy improved severe family maladaptation to chronic illness and significantly improved the child's adaptation to the illness as well as disease severity (Sargent, 1983). Gustaffson, Kjellman, and Cederblad (1986) tested the efficacy of structural family therapy for children with severe asthma. Compared with a no-treatment control condition, the children in the structural family therapy group demonstrated significant improvements in general pediatric assessment, peak expiratory flow, and medication adherence. Unfortunately, while particularly promising for children and adolescents, adaptation to chronic illness, there has been a dearth of research with *structural family therapy* for pediatric chronic illness populations over the last two decades.

Medical family therapy (MDFT) is a newly emerging specialty within the family therapy discipline that combines systems family therapy with the biopsychosocial paradigm of medicine to treat patients and families who are experiencing a physical or medical illness, trauma, or disability. The main tenet of medical family therapy is that biomedical events do not occur without psychosocial background and repercussions, and in turn, psychosocial events do not occur without some biological features (McDaniel, Hepworth, & Doherty, 1992). In this modality, therapists strive to work collaboratively with physicians and other health care providers in addressing the unique psychosocial problems of individuals, couples, and families with acute and chronic medically related concerns. Within the healthcare environment therapists provide psychosocial and spiritual services to those suffering with chronic illness. In addition, medical family therapists attempt to connect the family with the medical team in a manner that enables them to work together in a mutually supportive manner.

McDaniel and colleagues (1992) have described the specific goals of medical family therapy as including enhanced daily functioning for the patient and family, improved coping with chronic and acute symptoms related to illness, decreased conflict about treatment (e.g., managing medication), enhanced communication with healthcare providers, increased acceptance of a health problem that cannot be cured, and assistance in making necessary lifestyle changes due to an illness, such as diet or exercise. Unfortunately, despite the obvious appeal inherent in using medical family therapy to treat children and adolescents with chronic illness and their families, there are few empirical studies available demonstrating the efficacy of this technique for improving adherence, adaptation, and coping for children and adolescents with a chronic illness. This approach seems especially promising and awaits further empirical corroboration.

Nontraditional family-systems interventions also show promise for children and adolescents with chronic illness. For example, adolescents with diabetes and their families participated in a multifamily group designed to promote independent problem-solving skills and effective communication. The adolescents improved in metabolic control relative to a comparison group at the three- and six-month follow-up periods (Satin, La Greca, Zigo, & Skyler, 1989). However, no differences were found in adolescent's ratings of their parents' perceptions of family functioning. As another example, the efficacy of a "culturally and developmentally sensitive" intervention program for children with sickle cell disease and their low SES families was evaluated (Kaslow, Collins, Loundry, Brown, Hollins, & Eckman, 1997). There were few differences between the groups, although children participating in the experimental intervention group described themselves as being more improved and having increased knowledge of SCD in comparison with controls.

4.1.8   Parent Training

Parents are important change agents in promoting children's successful adaptation to chronic illness

Parent training is critical when working with children and adolescents with chronic illness. For example, parental involvement is often essential to insure adherence behaviors to children's and adolescent's treatment regimens, and to help generalize skills beyond the confines of psychotherapy. Kazak and colleagues (1996) completed a randomized controlled prospective outcome study of a combined psychological and pharmacological intervention relative to pharmacotherapy alone for procedurally related distress associated with the medical management of children with leukemia. The intervention instructed parents of younger children to assume the primary role in providing distraction, guided imagery, and externally oriented play. Child and parent psychological distress in both conditions was compared using mothers' and nurses' ratings. Both mothers and nurses rated children as less distressed in the treatment group that received a combined pharmacologic and psychological intervention relative to the group that received pharmacotherapy alone. The findings underscore the primary role of parents as change agents in promoting children's successful adaptation to these stressful disease-related procedures.

Summary

Family therapy is a particularly important psychosocial intervention because chronic illnesses impact the entire family, not just the child or adolescent. In addition, family members represent an important support system for the management of chronic illness. Evidence indicates that multisystemic family therapy and behavioral family systems therapy have demonstrated beneficial effects as intervention methods that improve adherence behaviors, health, and psychosocial outcomes in children and adolescents with chronic diseases. The evidence is less clear, however, for structural family therapy and medical family therapy.

4.1.9   Group Therapy

Children and adolescents with a chronic illness often are emotionally isolated, and group support helps diminish this burden. Group therapy provides participants with an opportunity to process personal issues with others who have similar experiences of living with a chronic illness. In addition, group experiences allow children and adolescents to become involved in a social situation and to see how their behavior affects others. The overarching goals of group therapy include assisting group members to develop new problem-solving and communication skills, social skills, and insights. The emphasis is placed on social support and mutual aid with other group members both providing and receiving help, while also serving as role models (Constantino & Nelson, 1995). In this manner, group interventions serve both psychoeducational and therapeutic functions.

Group therapies help children develop new problem-solving and communication skills, social skills, and insights

Group therapies, designed to be supportive and expressive, seek to develop supportive relationships among group members, enhance expression of emotional issues related to their illness, and build meaning in the face of the disease. Key issues that need to be addressed by group therapists include: (a) pregroup considerations such as assessment, selection issues with regard to membership in group, group composition, and determination of treatment goals; (b) establishing the group and difficulties associated with boundaries; and finally, (c) maintenance and termination issues (van Schoor, Schmidt, & Ghuman, 1998).

Plante, Lobato, and Engel (2001) completed an important meta-analysis of 125 studies between 1970 and 2000 that described group interventions for pediatric chronic conditions. The investigators classified the group interventions into four groups that were distinguished by their primary goals and intended outcomes: emotional support, psychoeducation, adaptation/skill development, or symptom reduction. Plante et al. also noted that summer camps are a form of group education. The main objective of emotional support groups is to improve psychological adaptation to illness by providing contact and discussion with others in similar situations so that group members and the therapist may help the children or adolescents manage the emotions they experience and offer them encouragement and comfort during difficult times. The hallmark of psychoeducational groups is education and information, which is provided to enhance psychological adjustment to the illness and its management as well as discussion of social and psychological issues. Goals associated with groups classified as adaptation/skill include the enhancement of psychosocial adaptation to the chronic illness and improved physical symptoms by enhancing specified skills. Finally, symptom reduction groups seek to reduce or eliminate physical symptoms through behavior change (Plante et al., 2001).

The studies reviewed by Plante et al. (2001) primarily included interventions for adolescents directed at increasing knowledge of illness, increasing psychological adaptation, and decreasing physical symptoms and adverse side effects associated with medical treatment. A major finding from this meta-analysis is that although well-established group interventions do exist for adaptation/skill development and symptom reduction, there is insufficient evidence to support the effectiveness of emotional support groups or psychoeducational groups. Specifically, adaptation and skill development are well-established interventions for physical symptoms, and are probably an efficacious intervention for psychosocial outcomes for children with diabetes and asthma. Symptom-reduction groups were classified as promising (e.g., cystic fibrosis) and a well-established treatment for conditions such as pediatric obesity and diabetes. However, there is a dearth of well-controlled studies to document the efficacy of emotional support groups. Overall, a significant gap continues to exist between what is clinically available in terms of group intervention for chronic illness and what is evidence-based (Plante et al., 2001).

Summer camps for children and adolescents with a chronic illness provide an important vehicle for participants to address those psychosocial needs associated with a chronic condition. In addition, camp participants often receive support from their peers who may have similar concerns about disease-specific problems such as illness experience and handling difficult situations with peers (e.g., dietary limitations among children with type I insulin-dependent diabetes). Beyond these factors, camps provide these children and adolescents with an opportunity to be in another environment, practice sports, and engage in activities and have fun with other children away from home and parents.

In the review by Plante and colleagues (2001), pre- and postevaluations of summer camp programs indicate that campers improved their disease-related knowledge and demonstrated improvements in self-esteem, anxiety, attitudes toward illness, and management of the disease. Briery and Rabian (1999) assessed the impact of specialized summer camps on children with spina bifida, asthma, and diabetes who went to camp at separate times. Significant improvements were found on standardized measures of anxiety and attitude. However, only children in the asthma and diabetes groups demonstrated decreases in anxiety over the course of the camp experience.

Health-related quality of life was measured in children and adolescents with inflammatory bowel disease (IBD) before and after attending an IBD summer camp (Shepanski, Hurd, Culton, Markowitz, Mamula, & Baldassano, 2005). Health-related quality of life generally improved in children after attending the IBD summer camp. The contributing factors for improvements may be associated with an increase in social functioning, a better acceptance of IBD symptoms, and less distress regarding treatment interventions. Thus, a specially designed camp experience for children with IBD may in fact "normalize" the chronic illness experience.

A review of nine published studies of recreation-based summer camps for children with cancer and their families found that such programs show at least short-term efficacy for increases in self-esteem, friendships, knowledge about cancer, level of activity, positive mood state, locus of control, and improved family functioning (Martiniuk, 2003). Moons et al. (2006) examined possible changes in the perceived health status and habitual physical activities in children with congenital heart disease attending a special sports camp. Improvements were noted in the children's perception of their physical functioning, role-physical functioning, general health, role-emotional functioning, self-esteem, mental health, and general functioning. At the three-month follow-up, high scores continued to persist for physical functioning, role-emotional functioning, and family activities. The findings of enhanced physical functioning are especially important given that children and adolescents with a chronic illness commonly experience restrictions in their daily activities and functional outcomes.

In one of the few studies that used a child-focused group intervention, Curle, Bradford, Thompson, and Cawthron (2005) investigated a brief group therapy intervention for children with chronic illness or disability, together with a parallel group for parents. The intervention, derived from Wallander and Varni's (1998) stress and coping model, was based on the assumption that enhanced coping and the facilitation of social support result would improve adaptation and enhance quality of life for children and their families. The specific targets of the intervention were the reduction of feelings of isolation and facilitation of coping among these youth. Children with chronic illness attended six to eight sessions of a highly structured, yet theoretically eclectic, group intervention. Simultaneously, parents attended a parallel group meeting that provided a therapeutic space for the parents' issues. Increased social support and enhanced emotion- and problem-focused coping responses were found for both child and parent groups. Specifically, qualitative data revealed that participants benefited from the intervention as a result of emotional support, connectedness with others who were coping with similar or more difficult circumstances, and giving and receiving practical advice about coping and problem-solving.

4.1.10 Peer Group Interventions

Recently there has been a burgeoning interest in peer group interventions and peer support programs for youth with chronic illness. Support groups enable children and adolescents with specific challenges to share experiences, information, and encouragement. Greco, Shroff-Pendley, McDonnell, and Reeves (2001), underscoring the importance of peer relationships during adolescence as a hallmark of development at this age period, developed a structured diabetes intervention that included adolescents' best friends and encouraged these peers to assist their friends with the diabetes regimen. The friends were taught to acquire and exhibit behaviors that are supportive and helpful in promoting effective diabetes self-care. The intervention included training in reflective listening and problem-solving, as well as general stress management. The target goals included increasing diabetes knowledge, enhancing communication skills, improving problem solving skills, and learning to manage stress. Findings revealed improvements in peers' knowledge about diabetes and ways in which to offer social support. Improved self-perception among peers also occurred as a function of the intervention program. In addition, parents reported a decline in diabetes-related family conflict. The results underscore the importance of peer support in promoting children and adolescents' successful adaptation to chronic illness.

4.1.11 Peer Support Groups

Peer support groups promote adherence, coping, and emotional well-being

Referring youth with a chronic illness to peer support groups for the purpose of promoting adherence, coping, and emotional well-being is gaining popularity as an alternative to the more conventional approaches of referring young people and their families to traditional mental health settings (Olsson, Sawyer, & Boyce, 2000). Funck-Bretano, Dalban, Veber, Quartier, Hefez, Costagliola, and Blanche (2005) conducted a prospective study of a cohort of HIV-infected adolescents participating or not participating in a psychodynamic oriented, emotional support group. The study involved 10 participants who received the peer support group, 10 participants who declined to participate, and 10 other HIV-infected youth who lived too far from the clinic and to participate. After two years, worries about illness had decreased in the active support group, whereas the scores had increased or remained the same for the adolescents in the other two nontreatment arms of the study. In addition, the adolescents in the active support group also had less negative perceptions of needing treatment at two years than those in the nontreatment groups. Finally, after intervention, the percentage of adolescents with an undetectable viral load (≤ 200 copies/ml) had increased in the active support group from 30% to 80% but was unchanged in the nontreatment groups. The investigators concluded that peer support group intervention is associated with an improvement in adolescents' emotional well being, and that this may have a positive influence on medical outcomes.

Olsson, Boyce, Toumbourou, and Sawyer (2005) recently described the development of a program, Chronic Illness Peer Support (ChIPS), which is intended to help young people (12–25 years) improve their social well-being and positively adjust to their life with any type of chronic illness or medical condition. The program uses a noncategorical approach and is based on the following aims for children and adolescents: (a) improve adjustment to living with a chronic illness; (b) develop a range of personal abilities; (c) increase a sense of control over their health status, and; (d) become more active in their local community. Additional aspects of ChIPS include the ability of graduates to train as peer facilitators and create an organized program of social events for all group participants (Olsson, Walsh, Toumbourou, & Bowes, 1997).

Olsson and Toumbourou (1996) identified nine psychosocial mechanisms through which peer support groups, including ChIPS, might serve to increase resilience and well-being among participants, including: (a) learning new coping techniques; (b) learning how to influence social environments; (c) enlarging perspectives on what is normal or typical; (d) examining alternative perspectives; (e) understanding the causes of personal stressors; (f) confirmation of positive changes in attitudes; (g) reducing a sense of isolation; (h) enhancing identity through group cohesion; and finally, (i) extending help to others. Although of theoretical interest, the ChIPS program and the proposed psychosocial mechanisms remain to be demonstrated empirically. Given the lack of empirical studies, it is premature to consider this peer-support program an evidence-based intervention.

4.1.12   Electronic Peer Support Groups

The research on nontraditional support groups has demonstrated mixed findings when used as a therapeutic intervention for youth with a chronic illness. For example, Johnson, Ravert, and Everton (2001) developed a web-based support service for adolescents with cystic fibrosis. The support group aimed to enhance children's relationships with the clinic faculty and staff, improve access to and interaction with peers with cystic fibrosis, and increase children's understanding of cystic fibrosis. The electronic support group proved to be effective in enhancing children's perception about their access to other teenagers with cystic fibrosis. However, there were no significant changes in perceptions about the perceived availability and comfort with the clinic staff and faculty, support available through peers, knowledge about cystic fibrosis, and the usefulness of the Internet as a support environment.

Another electronic support group is STARBRIGHT World, which is a private computer network that provides an opportunity for hospitalized children to interact with other hospitalized children in an online community. Evaluations of the STARBRIGHT program indicate that hospitalized children, ages 9 to 19, reported less pain intensity, pain aversiveness, and anxiety in the STARBRIGHT support group as compared to the normal pediatric care group (Holden, Bearison, Rode, Kapiloff, & Rosenberg, 2000; Holden, Bearison, Rode, Rosenberg, & Fishman, 1999).

Summary

Peer support groups and peer group interventions have generally demonstrated beneficial effects for many children and adolescents with chronic illnesses (Clark, Ichinose, Meseck-Bushey, Perez, Hall, Gibertini, & Crowe, 1992; Conway, Thompson, & Caldwell, 1996). More controlled trials are needed to document the value of peer group interventions prior to endorsing these approaches as efficacious.

4.1.13   Self-Regulatory Skill Training, Self-Management, and Psychoeducational Strategies

Chronic illnesses, particularly diabetes and asthma, typically require adherence to some type of treatment regimen and often involve self-monitoring of symptoms on the part of the child or adolescent. The goal of self-regulatory skills training is to convince children that they are able to effectively manage their illness (Fielding & Duff, 1999). Self-regulatory skills training includes self-regulation of medication, planning, and problem solving skills; training in intrapersonal and interpersonal skills; relapse prevention; and attribution retraining (Brownell & Cohen, 1995; Meichenbaum & Turk, 1987). Therapists initially seek to establish a collaborative relationship among health professionals, patients, and family members. Subsequently, therapists work with the multidisciplinary team caring for the child and family to define a single approach to their medical management, an approach that incorporates the self regulatory skills perspective (Fielding & Duff, 1999). Although much of the application of self-regulatory skills training has been conducted for adults with chronic disease, there is clear applicability for families of children with chronic illness (Fielding & Duff, 1999).

For children and adolescents with chronic disease, there is growing interest in "self-management" programs that emphasize the children's and adolescents' central role in managing as many aspects of their illness as possible. The primary aims of self-management programs are to enhance patients' skills with medical management, maintain life roles, and manage adjustment difficulties that might arise from such illness, including depressive symptoms as well as symptoms associated with anxiety. Children and adolescents with a chronic illness also are provided the knowledge, skills, and confidence necessary to negotiate illness-related problems. Similar to self-regulatory skills training, self-management programs prepare children and adolescents with a chronic illness to collaborate with their health care providers and overall health care system. Self-management support strategies include assessment of the problem, goal setting, action planning, problem-solving, decision making, confidence building, and follow-up. An example of a self-management intervention for pediatric asthma might include strategies such as appropriate use of medications to maintain a clear airway such as inhalers, identification of symptoms of an exacerbation, and avoidance of environmental triggers such as dust mites, pollen, or mold.

Psychoeducational strategies inform youth and their caregivers about the nature of chronic illness and its appropriate management

Psychoeducational strategies and intervention programs focus on providing verbal and written instructions to inform youth and their caregivers about the nature of the chronic illness and its appropriate management. These intervention programs are usually delivered in small groups and aim to effect change in knowledge of their disease and its appropriate management and behavior change through the development of self-management skills (Barlow, Shaw, & Harrison, 1999). Effects of psychoeducational interventions are believed to be mediated via their impact on individuals' self-efficacy, or perceived control over their disease process (Bandura 1997).

An example of a comprehensive psychoeducational program for children and adolescents with chronic illness is the Cystic Fibrosis Family Education Program, which focuses on the improvement of adherence to self-management of a specific disease regimen for cystic fibrosis across the entire treatment regimen (Bartholomew et al., 1997). This program uses a self-paced curriculum that provides teaching on the multiple aspects involved with self-management in cystic fibrosis (CF) and instructs families on the use of goal-setting, reinforcement, and self-monitoring (Spirito & Kazak, 2006). The program covers both the medical and psychosocial aspects of CF and includes four educational content areas: (a) respiratory problems; (b) nutrition; (c) communication; and finally, (d) coping with the disease.

Bartholomew and colleagues (1997) conducted a study to test the efficacy of the program and reported improved knowledge scores for caregivers, adolescents, and children. In addition, improvements were reported in caregiver and adolescent total self-management scores. In contrast, Goldbeck and Babka (2001) evaluated the impact of a psychoeducational program for families with a child affected by CF and found no changes on measures of adherence or coping.

Bonner, Zimmerman, Evans, Irigoyen, Resnick, and Mellins (2002) conducted a randomized controlled trial to evaluate the efficacy of an educational intervention based on a readiness model to improve asthma management among urban Latino and African-American families. The investigators identified four sequential phases of the readiness to manage asthma model, including: (a) asthma symptom avoidance; (b) asthma acceptance; (c) asthma compliance; and finally, (d) asthma self-regulation. A "family coordinator" served as a behavioral change agent who delivered patient education through educational workshops and individualized counseling sessions that used an asthma diary as a primary intervention tool. Families in the intervention group, compared to families in the control group, demonstrated improved knowledge of asthma, more positive health beliefs, increased self-efficacy, enhanced self-regulatory skills, and better adherence. Additional findings included decreased symptom persistence, enhanced activity, and more frequent prescription of anti-inflammatory medication by the physicians of the intervention group families.

Velsor-Friedrich, Pigott, and Srof (2005) also evaluated the impact of African-American inner-city children's participation in an asthma education program (Open Airways), followed by five monthly visits with a nurse practitioner. Children in the active treatment group scored significantly higher than the control group over time on measures of asthma knowledge, asthma self-efficacy, general self-care practices, and asthma self-care practices. However, significant differences were not found between the two groups on health outcomes.

Barlow and Ellard (2004) reviewed the research evidence base for psychoeducational interventions for children with chronic disease. They reviewed 12 intervention studies that included: chronic disease in general ($n = 3$); chronic pain ($n = 1$); asthma ($n = 3$); chronic fatigue syndrome (CFS)/myalgic encephalomyelitis (ME) ($n = 1$); diabetes ($n = 2$); juvenile idiopathic arthritis (JIA) ($n = 1$) and one informational intervention for pediatric cancer patients. In brief, findings supported the effectiveness of interventions incorporating cognitive-behavioral techniques on variables such as self-efficacy, self-management of disease, family functioning, psychosocial well-being, reduced isolation, social competence, knowledge, hope, pain (for chronic headache), lung function (asthma), days absent from school (asthma), fatigue (chronic fatigue syndrome), and metabolic control (diabetes).

4.2   Mechanisms of Action

Interestingly, relatively little is known about the specific mechanisms of action that actually produce therapeutic change in psychosocial intervention trials. Although there is strong evidence for the efficacy of certain randomized controlled trials, the biobehavioral and psychosocial mechanisms of action in which the intervention operates are less clear. Examples of proposed mechanisms of action include parent and child expectancies for treatment, therapeutic alliance, and other 'common factors' (Kazdin & Nock, 2003).

Weersing and Weisz (2002) reviewed the literature on mechanisms of action in empirically supported treatments used in child and adolescent psychotherapy. They concluded that clinical trials of empirically supported treatments for youth who are anxious and phobic, depressed, or disruptive, provide only limited information on possible mechanisms of therapeutic action. In addition, Kazdin and Nock (2003) propose that research designs (e.g., randomized controlled trials, pretest/posttest designs) as they are currently employed, fail to adequately evaluate mechanisms of action. For this reason, an increased focus on studying mechanisms of action to understand the specific components of psychotherapy that produce improvement, how improvement occurs and why some individuals do not respond to specific components of psychotherapy has been recommended (Kazdin & Nock, 2003).

4.3   Efficacy and Prognosis

Beale (2006) recently completed a comprehensive literature review of the efficacy of psychological interventions for pediatric chronic illness. Specific types of pediatric chronic illness included diabetes, cancer, cystic fibrosis, and sickle cell disease. Methods of therapy in the intervention studies included cognitive-behavior therapy, biofeedback training, hypnosis, and interactive computer games or educational tutorials specifically tailored to match the various illness categories. The review identified 19 studies that provided data on 62 outcome variables.

Research suggests that psychological interventions for pediatric chronic illness are generally efficacious

Adjunctive psychological interventions for pediatric chronic illness were associated with large effect sizes, indicating that the interventions were generally efficacious. Specifically, results indicated that the mean effect size across all active intervention conditions was 0.71 (range = 0.28–3.23, SD = 0.61), whereas the mean effect size for control conditions was 0.12 (range = 0.82–0.87, SD = 0.39). Effect sizes were based on difference between pre- and postintervention means in the treatment group. Associations between effect size and illness type did not demonstrate that larger effect sizes were related to specific illness types. For example, findings revealed the following mean effect sizes for each illness category: sickle cell disease, 0.77 (SD = 0.56);

cancer, 0.56 ($SD = 0.77$); diabetes and cystic fibrosis, 0.88 ($SD = 0.75$), suggesting that effect sizes ranged from medium to large. Diversity of intervention methods and content did not allow for an analysis of effects size by intervention type. Although medium to large effect sizes were found for psychological interventions for pediatric chronic illness, Beale (2006) cautions that more studies are needed before it is possible to unequivocally proclaim the overwhelming efficacy of such interventions.

Wolf, Guevara, Grum, Clark, and Cates (2003) conducted a meta-analysis of educational interventions employed for children with asthma. An overall mean effect size of 0.30 was found, when the effect size was based on the difference between postintervention means for the treatment group versus the control group. In another meta-analysis that investigated the effectiveness of psychological interventions for pediatric chronic illness, Kibby, Tyc, and Mulhern (1998) reported an overall mean effect size of 0.87 for treatment versus control comparisons and 1.4 for pre-post comparisons. It is noteworthy that treatment gains were maintained for at least 12 months following the conclusion of the treatment. Interventions for disease management and emotional/behavioral problems were found to be effective for children and adolescents with a chronic illness. Similar to the findings from Beale's (2006) meta-analysis, Kibby et al. (1998) did not report any significant differences across effect sizes as a function of the type of intervention or the type of outcome measure.

4.4   Variations and Combinations of Methods

Combining traditional psychological intervention methods have become more common in the psychosocial treatment of children and adolescent with chronic illness. Examples of combined treatment approaches include educational-behavioral interventions, behavioral family systems therapy, behavioral-psychopharmacological approaches, educational-supportive therapy, group family cognitive-behavioral interventions, and multifamily group therapy. Combined therapies offer the advantage of addressing multiple challenges faced by the child and family including medical adherence difficulties, psychological and psychosocial stressors, and quality of life issues. Although there is evidence for the effectiveness of multimodal therapies for childhood depression, anxiety, and ADHD, no clinical trials have been conducted that compare monotherapy to combination therapies for children and adolescents with chronic illness.

4.5   Problems in Carrying Out the Treatment

Barriers to psychosocial treatment of children and adolescents with chronic illness include individual, family, provider, and setting and system-based challenges. Identifying and overcoming these barriers is important given the evidence indicating that children with chronic physical illness who have a diagnosable mental health disorder vastly underutilize psychological services (Cadman, Boyle, Szatmari, & Offord, 1987).

Barriers to treatment include individual, family, provider, and system and setting-based barriers

4.5.1   Individual Barriers

Approximately one half of pediatric patients with chronic illness are considered nonadherent to medical treatment recommendations (Rapoff & Barnard, 1991). Common individual barriers include forgetting, oppositional behaviors, difficulties with time management, limited resources, inadequate knowledge about the disease and appropriate management, and psychosocial resistance to adhering to a disease regimen due to avoidance of the disease (denial), peer conformity in adolescence, etc. (Koocher, McGrath, & Gudas, 1990; Modi & Quittner, 2006). Adherence behaviors may be improved by designing interventions that match the specific barriers that interfere with children's and adolescents' medical management.

4.5.2   Family Barriers

There is compelling evidence to indicate that parents of children with chronic illness are at risk for emotional distress and problems with adjustment as a result of the multiple stressors and additional burdens associated with caring for children with a chronic health condition (Wallander & Varni, 1998). In addition, siblings of children with a chronic illness are at risk for negative psychological sequelae (Sharpe & Rossiter, 2002). Families who become overwhelmed with these stressors and burdens may experience difficulty initiating or maintaining their participation in psychological interventions. This problem may be addressed by including families in the treatment process as well as providing them with information and support about the illness.

4.5.3   Provider Barriers

The literature on provider barriers for children with chronic conditions is decidedly mixed. Sabbeth and Stein (1990) suggest that interventions for families with children with chronic medical conditions can be more difficult to deliver, compared to interventions for children without medical difficulties. In addition, Glazebrook, Hollis, Heussler, Goodman, and Coates (2003) reported that primary care physicians under identify psychosocial concerns among children with chronic conditions. In contrast to these findings, Bilfield, Wildman, and Karazsia (2006) recently examined data pertaining to primary care physicians' identification and management of pediatric chronic illness and found that providers identified psychosocial concerns in significantly more children with a chronic illness (38.6%) than healthy children (20.2%), with no differences reported for rates of identification, treatment, and barriers to treatment between the two groups.

4.5.4   System and Setting-Based Barriers

Another barrier to carrying out psychosocial treatments is system-based obstacles (e.g., lack of third-party reimbursement) that may limit providers' attempts to use medically indicated psychological services for various pediatric chronic illnesses (see Taylor et al., 2006). Providers are encouraged to advocate for appropriate reimbursement for services that address children's physical and mental health.

Lastly, the location and hours of operation of mental health services may present challenges to some youth and their families; For example, some clinics are only open during school hours. Service provision during evening or weekend hours may improve families' ability to utilize mental health services. In addition, there has been a recent surge in the application of distance treatments, such as those delivered over the Internet or by telephone. These alternative applications of service delivery may offer significant promise for rural and other underserved populations, as they expand both provider and client access to health care (Devineni & Blanchard, 2005; Jerome & Zaylor, 2000). For example, the Starlight-Starbright Foundation (www.starlight.org) has been developing programs that help the participating children comply with their treatment, cope with pain, understand their illness, and communicate clearly with their physicians (Bush, Huchital, & Simonian, 2002).

4.6   Multicultural Issues

Sifers, Puddy, Warren, & Roberts (2002) reviewed articles in major journals of clinical child and pediatric psychology to determine the rate at which demographic variables are reported, (e.g., socioeconomic status, ethnicity). Findings indicate that participants' ethnicity was reported in 63.1% of articles that were reviewed, while socioeconomic status was reported in only about half the studies. Unfortunately, missing ethnicity and socioeconomic data restricts our ability to determine how to apply the results to specific ethnic or cultural groups.

Clay, Mordhorst, and Lehn (2002) conducted a review of studies used to support empirically supported treatments for asthma, cancer, diabetes, and obesity in order to examine whether the studies addressed issues of cultural diversity (e.g., race/ethnicity, SES). These illness conditions were chosen to due their strong link to race, ethnicity, and culture. Findings revealed that 27% of the studies reported the race or ethnicity, 18% reported the SES of research participants, and only 6% discussed potential moderating cultural variables. The authors interpret these findings to suggest that empirically supported treatments do not adequately address important issues of culture. Clay et al. interpret their findings and suggest questionable external validity of empirically supported treatments to diverse populations.

Fortunately, several recent intervention studies have been completed with children and adolescents with chronic illness from specific ethnic minority groups. For example, Velsor-Friedrich et al. (2005) conducted a practitioner-based asthma intervention with African-American inner-city school children. In addition, Bonner and colleagues (2002) conducted individualized interventions to improve asthma management among urban Latino and African-American families. Nonetheless, it is clear that evidence is lacking to document the effectiveness of empirically supported interventions with respect to children and families from diverse cultural and socioeconomic backgrounds.

Multicultural issues have not been adequately addressed for empirically supported treatments for pediatric chronic illnesses

Future research needs to target diverse groups of parents and their children in order to determine what types of interventions work for which groups of people.

4.7   Summary

The overwhelming majority of children and adolescents with chronic illness are living into adulthood due in large measure to advancements in medical technology. With the improved survival rate, mental health providers find themselves on the front-line engaging in interventions that address issues of quality of life, psychological adjustment, adherence, coping, and psychosocial factors. The various types of interventions employed with these children, adolescents, and their families include psychoeducation, parent training, and individual, family, peer, and group therapies. The health care and psychological literatures offer considerable evidence to support the efficacy of psychological interventions in pediatric chronic illness (Beale, 2006). In general these intervention studies have provided support for the correlation studies that previously had been conducted with children and adolescents with chronic illness. Nonetheless, more research needs to investigate which types of interventions maximize the physical and biological outcomes as well as the quality of life of these children, adolescents, and their families.

Case Vignette

Cassandra is a 16-year-old Caucasian female who was seen at a mental health clinic because of her depressed mood. Her mother was referred to the clinic by Cassandra's pediatrician and indicated that her daughter has had a history of depression since she was in kindergarten. In addition, Cassandra has a history of cystic fibrosis since she was three years old and has been hospitalized frequently for the condition.

Cassandra lives with her mother and younger brother. She reported that her parents are divorced because her father drinks a lot and cannot keep a job. Cassandra does see her father occasionally but not as often as she would like. On occasion she has reported feeling sad after visiting with her father. Her mother is an attorney and is the sole supporter of the family.

In the past few months, Cassandra revealed that she has not been sleeping very well and has no appetite. She has dropped out of extracurricular activities at school complaining that she is tired, and also has been expressing the feeling that no one likes her. Cassandra's mother also reported that there has been a significant decline in school work with her even failing to complete assignments. Due to her frequent hospitalizations for cystic fibrosis, Cassandra has always been behind in her academic work. Her mother has hired tutors from time to time to help Cassandra with her school work. At age 13, Cassandra attempted suicide by overdosing on illicit drugs which led to psychiatric hospitalization. Upon discharge, she became involved in psychotherapy for approximately one year.

During the interview, Cassandra appeared melancholy and at times started crying. She said her boyfriend has just broken up with her and this was the reason she was so unhappy. Cassandra indicated this was another example of no one liking her.

After the case consultation, Cassandra was diagnosed with major depressive disorder. She was given antidepressant medication (5 mg escitalopram) and the recommendation of the psychiatrist was for Cassandra to become involved in cognitive behavior therapy and family therapy.

It has been suggested by several investigators that the psychological adjustment of children with cystic fibrosis is different than that of healthy individuals. Researchers have reportedly found significantly higher incidences of eating disorders, depression, and anxiety in this population. While major advances have been made in the medical treatment of cystic fibrosis that has resulted in a longer life expectancy, similar advances have not been made with regard to psychological interventions. Most interventions that have been labeled psychological are actually educational and deal with treatment to enhance adaptation. Clinical trials need to be conducted that evaluate which psychological interventions are most effective in helping individuals and families deal with the consequences of psychiatric comorbidities. Furthermore, psychotropic medications utilized for emotional problems such as depression have also not been appropriately evaluated with chronic illness populations including cystic fibrosis.

6

Further Reading

This section includes key references to literature where the practitioner can find further details or background information.

Drotar, D. (Ed.) (2000). *Promoting adherence to medical treatment in chronic childhood illness: Concepts, methods, and interventions*. Mahwah, NJ: Laurence Erlbaum.
   The content of this book is derived from presentations at a conference held at Case Western Reserve University that assembled experts in the field of pediatric compliance in chronic illness. This edited book includes information on the conceptual models of adherence as well as patient-centered and self-management approaches to adherence.
Drotar, D. (2006). *Psychological interventions in childhood chronic illness*. Washington, DC: American Psychological Association.
   This comprehensive book reviews the most current psychological intervention research for children with chronic illness. In particular, it examines psychological interventions for asthma, diabetes, pediatric cancer, sickle cell disease, juvenile rheumatoid arthritis, and cystic fibrosis. This book also reviews pragmatic strategies for conducting research and interventions with this population.
Roberts, M. C. (2003). *Handbook of pediatric psychology*. New York: The Guilford Press.
   This comprehensive handbook has five major sections: (a) professional issues; (b) cross-cutting issues in pediatric psychology; (c) chronic medical conditions: research and clinical applications; (d) developmental, behavioral, and cognitive/affective conditions; and (e) emerging issues. This edited handbook brings together contributions from the leading pediatric psychology clinicians and researchers. Although each chapter is focused, the breadth of this book is impressive.
Thompson, R. J., & Gustafson, K. E. (1996). *Adaptation to chronic childhood illness*. Washington, DC: American Psychological Association.
   This seminal work is the major source for information about adaptation and psychological adjustment to childhood chronic illness. Although the research citations are somewhat dated, this excellent text includes sections on the impact of chronic childhood illness, developmental changes, enhancing adaptation, and goals for public policy and research. The book provides thorough discussions of treatment issues and is particularly applicable for social scientists and health care professionals who care for children with chronic illness.

7

References

Achenbach, T. M. (1991). *Child Behavior Checklist and Child Behavior Profile: Cross-Informant Version*. Burlington, VT: University of Vermont.

Akinbami, L. J., LaFleur, B. J., & Schoendorf, K. C. (2002). Racial and income disparities in childhood asthma in the United States. *Ambulatory Pediatrics, 2*, 382–387.

American Psychiatric Association. (2000). *Diagnostic and statistical manual of mental disorders* (4th ed., text revision). Washington, DC: Author.

Anderson, D. L., Brown, R. T., & Williams, L. (1999). Summaries, training, ethics, and direction. In R. T. Brown (Ed.), *Cognitive aspects of chronic illness in children* (pp. 386–406). New York: Guilford Press.

Armstrong, F. D., Toledano, S. R., Miloslavich, K., Lackman-Zeman, L., Levy, J. D., Gay, C. L., et al. (1999). The Miami Pediatric Quality Of Life Questionnaire: Parent Scale. *International Journal of Cancer, 12*(supplement), 11–17.

Aylward, G. P. (2003). Cognitive function in preterm infants: No simple answers. *Journal of the American Medical Association, 289*, 752–753.

Ballas, S. (1991). Sickle cell anemia with few painful crises is characterized by decreased red cell deformability and increased number of dense cells. *American Journal of Hematology, 36*, 122–130.

Bandura, A. (1997) Self-efficacy: The exercise of control. New York: W. H. Freeman and Company.

Barkley, R. A., Guevremont, D. C., Anastopoulous, A. D., & Fletcher, K. E. (1992). A comparison of three family therapy programs for treating family conflicts in adolescents with attention-deficit/hyperactivity disorder. *Journal of Consulting and Clinical Psychology, 60*, 450–462.

Barlow, J. H., & Ellard, D. R. (2004). Psycho-educational interventions for children with chronic disease, parents, and siblings: An overview of the research evidence base. *Child: Care, Health, and Development, 30*, 637–645.

Barlow, J. H., & Ellard, D. R. (2006). The psychosocial well-being of children with chronic disease, their parents, and siblings: An overview of the research evidence base. *Child: Care, Health, and Development, 32*, 19–31.

Barlow, J. H., & Shaw, K. L., & Harrison, K. (1999). Consulting the "experts:" Children and parents' perceptions of psychoeducational interventions in the context of juvenile arthritis. *Health Education Research, 14*, 597–610.

Bartholomew, L. K, Czyzewski, D. I., Parcel, G. S., Swank, P. R., Sockrider, M. M., Mariotto, M. J., et al. (1997). Self-management of cystic fibrosis: Short-term outcomes of the cystic fibrosis family education program. *Health Education and Behavior, 24*, 652–666.

Bartlett, S. J., Lukk, P., Butz, A., Lampros-Klein, F., & Rand, C. S. (2002). Enhancing medication adherence among inner-city children with asthma: Results from pilot studies. *Journal of Asthma, 39*, 47–54.

Bauman, L. J., Drotar, D., Leventhal, J. M., Perrin, E. C., & Pless, I. B. (1997). A review of psychosocial interventions for children with chronic health conditions. *Pediatrics, 100*, 244–251.

Beale, I. L. (2006). Scholarly literature review: Efficacy of psychological interventions for pediatric chronic illness. *Journal of Pediatric Psychology, 31,* 437–451.

Beale, I. L., Bradlyn, A. S., & Kato, P. M. (2003). Psychoeducational interventions with pediatric cancer patients: Part II. Effects of knowledge and skills training on health-related attitudes and behavior. *Journal of Child and Family Studies, 20*, 385–397.

Beck, J. S., Beck, A. T., & Jolly, J. B. (2001). *Beck youth inventories.* San Antonio, TX: The Psychological Corporation.

Belar, C. D., & Deardorff, W. W. (1995). *Clinical health psychology in medical settings: A practitioner's guidebook.* (2nd ed.). Washington, DC: American Psychological Association.

Bender, B. G., Annett, R. D., Ikle, D., DuHamel, T. R., Rand, C., & Strunk, R. C. (2000). Relationship between disease and psychological adaptation in children in the Childhood Asthma Management Program and their families. *Archives of Pediatric and Adolescent Medicine, 154*, 706–713.

Bennett, D. S. (1994). Depression among children with chronic medical problems: A meta-analysis. *Journal of Pediatric Psychology, 19*, 149–169.

Berry, R. J., Buehler, J. W., Strauss, L. T., Hogue, C. J. R., & Smith, J. C. (1987). Birth weight-specific infant mortality due to congenital anomalies, 1960 and 1980. *Public Health Reports, 102*, 171–181.

Bilfield, S., Wildman, B. G., & Karazsia, B. T. (2006). Brief Report: The relationship between chronic illness and identification and management of psychosocial problems in pediatric primary care. *Journal of Pediatric Psychology, 31,* 813–817.

Blanz, B., Rensch-Riemann, B., Fritz-Sigmund, D., & Schmidt, M. (1993). IDDM is a risk factor for adolescent psychiatric disorders. *Diabetes Care, 16,* 1579–1587.

Bonner, M. J., Hardy, K. K., Guill, A. B., McLaughlin, C., Schweitzer, H., & Carter, K. (2005). Development and validation of the parent experience of child illness. *Journal of Pediatric Psychology, 31,* 310–321.

Bonner, S., Zimmerman, B. J., Evans, D., Irigoyen, M., Resnick, D., & Mellins, R. B. (2002). An individualized intervention to improve asthma management among urban Latino and African-American families. *Journal of Asthma, 39,* 167–179.

Braswell, L., & Kendall, P. C. (1988). Cognitive-behavioral methods with children. In K. Dobson (Ed.), *Handbook of cognitive-behavioral therapies* (pp. 167–213). New York: Guilford.

Braswell, L., & Kendall, P. C. (2001). Cognitive-behavioral therapy with children. In K. Dobson (Ed.), *Handbook of cognitive-behavioral therapies* (2nd ed., pp. 246–294). New York: Guilford.

Briery, B. G., & Rabian, B. (1999). Psychosocial changes associated with participation in a pediatric summer camp. *Journal of Pediatric Psychology, 24,* 183–190.

Broome, M. E., Maikler, V., Kelber, S., Bailey, P., & Lea, G. (2001). An intervention to increase coping and reduce health care utilization for school-age children and adolescents with sickle cell disease. *Journal of the National Black Nurses Association, 12,* 6–14.

Brown, R. T. (2006). Chronic illness and neurodevelopmental disability. In J. E. Farmer, J. Donders, & S. Warschausky (Eds.), *Treating neurodevelopmental disabilities: Clinical research and practice* (pp. 98–118). New York: Guilford Publications.

Brown, R. T., Davis, P. C., Lambert, R., Hsu, L., Hopkins, K., & Eckman, J. R. (2000). Neurocognitive functioning and magnetic resonance imaging in children with sickle cell disease. *Journal of Pediatric Psychology, 25,* 503–513.

Brown, R. T., Dingle, A. D., & Dreelin, E. (1997). Neuropsychological effects of stimulant medication on children's learning and behavior. In C. R. Reynolds & E. Fletcher-Janzen (Eds.), *Handbook of clinical child neuropsychology* (pp. 539–572). New York: Plenum Press.

Brown, R. T., Doepke, K. J., & Kaslow, N. J. (1993). Risk-resistance-adaptation model for pediatric chronic illness: Sickle cell syndrome as an example. *Clinical Psychology Review, 13,* 119–132.

Brown, R. T., Eckman, J., Baldwin, K., Buchanan, I., & Dingle, A. D. (1995). Protective aspects of adaptive behavior in children with sickle cell syndromes. *Children's Health Care, 24,* 205–222.

Brown, R. T., & Macias, M. (2001). *Chronically ill children and adolescents.* In J. Hughes, A. La Greca, & J. C. Conoley (Eds.), *Handbook of psychological services to children and adolescents* (pp. 353–372). New York: Oxford.

Brown, R. T., Madan-Swain, A., & Lambert, R. (2003). Posttraumatic stress symptoms in adolescent survivors of childhood cancer and their mothers. *Journal of Traumatic Stress, 16,* 309–318.

Brownbridge, G., & Fielding, D. (1991). Psychosocial adjustment to end stage renal failure comparing haemodialysis, continuous ambulatory peritoneal dialysis, and transplantation. *Pediatric Nephrology, 5*, 612–616.

Brownell, K. D., & Cohen, L. R. (1995). Adherence to dietary regimens 2: Components of effective interventions. *Behavioral Medicine, 20*, 155–164.

Burlew, K., Telfair, J., Colangelo, L., & Wright, E. (2000). Factors that influence adolescent adaptation to sickle cell disease. *Society of Pediatric Psychology, 25*, 287–299.

Bush, J. P., Huchital, J. R., & Simonian, S. J. (2002). An introduction to program and research initiatives of the STARBRIGHT foundation. *Children's Health Care, 31*, 1–10.

Cadman, D. T., Boyle, M. H., Szatmari, P., & Offord, D. R. (1987). Chronic illness, disability, and mental and social well-being: Findings of the Ontario Child Health Study. *Pediatrics, 79*, 805–813.

Campo, J. V., & Fritsch, S. L. (1994). Somatization in children and adolescents. *Journal of the American Academy of Child and Adolescent Psychiatry, 33*, 1223–1235.

Canning, E. H., & Kelleher, K. (1994). Performance of screening tools for mental health problems in chronically ill children. *Archives of Pediatrics and Adolescent Medicine, 148*, 272–278.

Casey, F. A., Sykes, D. H., Craig, B. G., Power, R., & Mulholland, H. C. (1996). Behavioral adjustment of children with surgically palliated complex congenital heart disease. *Journal of Pediatric Psychology, 21*, 335–352.

Casey, R., Brown, R. T., & Bakeman, R. (2000). Predicting adjustment in children and adolescents with sickle cell disease: A test of the risk-resistance-adaptation model. *Rehabilitation Psychology, 45*, 155–178.

Castes, M., Hagel, I., Palenque, M., Canelones, P., Corao, A., & Lynch, N. R. (1999). Immunological changes associated with clinical improvement of asthmatic children subjected to psychosocial intervention. *Brain, Behavior, and Immunity, 13*, 1–13.

Cecalupo, A. (1994). Childhood cancers. Medical issues. In R. A. Olson, L. L. Mullins, J. B. Gillman, & J. M. Chaney (Eds.), *The sourcebook of pediatric psychology* (pp. 90–97). Boston: Allyn & Bacon.

Centers for Disease Control and Prevention. (1996). Asthma morbidity and hospitalization among children with young adults: US 1980–1993. *Morbidity and Mortality Weekly, 45*, 350–353.

Centers for Disease Control and Prevention. (2000). Measuring childhood asthma prevalence before and after the 1997 redesign of the National Health Institute survey – United States. *Morbidity and Mortality Weekly Report, 49*, 908–911.

Centers for Disease Control and Prevention. (2003). 2001 National Health Interview Survey (NHIS): Public use data release. Retrieved April 4, 2007, from http://www.cdc.gov/nchs/about/major/nhis/quest_data_related_1997_forward.htm.

Charache, S., Lubin, B., & Reid, C. (1989). Management and therapy of sickle cell disease. (NIH Publication No. 89-2117). Washington, DC: National Institute of Health.

Chasnoff, I. J., Griffith, D. R., Freier, C., & Murray, J. (1992). Cocaine/polydrug use in pregnancy: Two-year follow-up. *Pediatrics, 89*, 284–289.

Chen, E., Cole, S. W., & Kato, P. M. (2004). A review of empirically supported psychosocial interventions for pain and adherence outcomes in sickle cell disease. *Journal of Pediatric Psychology, 29,* 197–209.

Clark, H. B., Ichinose, C. K., Meseck-Bushey, S., Perez, K. R., Hall, M. S., Gibertini, M., & Crowe, T. (1992). Peer support group for adolescents with chronic illness. *Child Health Care, 21*, 233–238.

Clark, N. M., Gong, M., & Kaciroti, N. (2001). A model of self-regulation for control of chronic disease. *Health Education and Behavior, 28*, 769–782.

Clay, D. L., Mordhorst, M. J., & Lehn, L. (2002). Empirically supported treatments in pediatric psychology: Where is the diversity? *Journal of Pediatric Psychology, 27*, 325–338.

Collins, M., Kaslow, N., Doepke, K., Eckman, J., & Johnson, J. (1998). Psychosocial interventions for children and adolescents with sickle cell disease (SCD). *Journal of Black Psychology, 24,* 432–454.

Conners, C. K. (1997). *Conners' Rating Scales – Revised.* Toronto: Multi-Health Systems Inc.

Constantino, V., & Nelson, G. (1995) Changing relationships between self-help groups and mental health professionals: Shifting ideology and power. *Canadian Journal of Community Mental Health, 14*, 55–70.

Conway, C., Thompson, E., & Caldwell, C. (1996). Peer support group for adolescents. *Paediatric Nursing, 8*, 13–16.

Cook, S., Herold, K. C., Edidin, D. V., & Briars, R. (2002). Increasing problem-solving in adolescents with type 1 diabetes: The choices diabetes program. *The Diabetes Educator, 28*, 115–124.

Crain, E. F., Kercsmar, C., Weiss, K. B., Mitchell, H., & Lynn, H. (1998). Reported difficulties in access to quality care for children with asthma in the inner city. *Archives of Pediatrics and Adolescent Medicine, 152*, 333–339.

Cramer, J., Westbrook, L., Devinsky, O., Perrine, K., Glassman, M. B., & Camfield, C. (1999). Development of the quality of life in epilepsy inventory for adolescents: The QOLIE-AD-48. *Epilepsia, 40*, 1114–1121.

Curle, C., Bradford, J., Thompson, J., & Cawthron, P. (2005). Users' views of a group therapy intervention for chronically ill or disabled children and their parents: Towards a meaningful assessment of therapeutic effectiveness. *Clinical Child Psychology and Psychiatry, 10*, 509–527.

Cystic Fibrosis Foundation. (2003). Patient registry 2002 annual data report. Bethesda, MD: Author.

Czyzewski, D. I., & Bartholomew, K. (1998). Quality of life outcomes in children and adolescents with cystic fibrosis. In D. Drotar (Ed), *Measuring health-related quality of life in children and adolescents* (pp. 203–218). Mahwah, NJ: Lawrence Erlbaum Associates.

Davis, H., Schoendorf, K. C., Gergen, P. J., & Moore, R. M. (1997). National trends in the mortality of children with sickle cell disease: 1968 through 1992. American Journal of Public Health*, 87*, 1317–1322.

Devineni, T., & Blanchard, E. B. (2005). A randomized controlled trial of an internet-based treatment for chronic headache. *Behavior Research Therapy, 43*, 277–292.

DiGirolamo, A. M., Quittner, A. L., Ackerman, V., & Stevens, J. (1997). Identification and assessment of ongoing stressors in adolescents with a chronic illness: An application of the behavior analytic model. *Journal of Clinical Child Psychology, 26*, 53–66.

Drotar, D. (1997). Relating parent and family functioning to the psychological adjustment of children with chronic health conditions: What have we learned? What do we need to know? *Journal of Pediatric Psychology, 22*, 149–165.

Drotar, D. (2006). *Psychological interventions in childhood chronic illness.* Washington, DC: American Psychological Association.

Egger, H. L., Costello, E. J., Erkanli, A., & Angold, A. (1999). Somatic complaints and psychopathology in children and adolescents: Stomach aches, musculoskeletal pains, and headaches. *Journal of the American Academy of Child and Adolescent Psychiatry, 38*, 852–860.

Eiser, C. (1990). *Chronic childhood disease: An introduction to psychological theory and research.* Cambridge, UK: Cambridge University Press.

Eiser, C., Hill, J. J., & Vance, Y. H. (2000). Examining the psychological consequences of surviving childhood cancer: Systematic review as a research method in pediatric psychology. *Journal of Pediatric Psychology, 25*, 449–460.

Ellis, D. A., Frey, M. A., Naar-King, S., Templin, T., Cunningham, P. B., & Cakan, N. (2005). Use of multisystemic therapy to improve regimen adherence among adolescents with type 1 diabetes in chronic poor metabolic control: A randomized controlled trial. *Diabetes Care, 28*, 1604–1610.

Ellis, D. A., Narr-King, S., Cunningham, P. B., & Secord, E. (2006). Use of multisystemic therapy to improve antiretroviral adherence and health outcomes in HIV-infected pediatric patients: Evaluation of a pilot program. *AIDS, Patient Care, and STDs, 20*, 112–121.

Ellis, D. A., Naar-King, S., Frey, M., Rowland, M. D., & Greger, N. (2003). Case study: Feasibility of multisystemic therapy as a treatment for urban adolescents with poorly controlled type 1 diabetes. *Journal of Pediatric Psychology, 28,* 287–293.

Ellis, D. A., Naar-King, S., Frey, M., Templin, T., Rowland, M. D., & Cakan, N. (2005). Multisystemic treatment of poorly controlled type 1 diabetes: Effects on medical resource utilization. *Journal of Pediatric Psychology, 30,* 656–666.

Eminson, D. M., Benjamin, S., Shortall, A., Woods, T., & Faragher, B. (1996). Physical symptoms and illness attitudes in adolescents: An epidemiological study. *Journal of Child Psychology and Psychiatry, 37,* 519–527.

Erickson, S. J., & Steiner, H. (2001). Trauma and personality correlates in long term pediatric cancer survivors. *Child Psychiatry and Human Development, 31,* 195–213.

Evans, I. (1992). Asthma among minority children: A growing problem. *Chest, 101,* 368S–371S.

Evans, R., Mullaly, D. I., Wilson, R. W., Gergen, P. J., Rosenberg, H. M., Grauman, J. S., et al. (1987). Prevalence, hospitalization and death from asthma over two decades: 1965–1984. *Chest, 91,* 65S–74S.

Festa, R. S., Tamaroff, M. H., Chasalow, F., & Lanzkowsky, P. (1992). Therapeutic adherence to oral medication regimens by adolescents with cancer I. Laboratory assessment. *Journal of Pediatrics, 120,* 807–811.

Fielding, D., & Duff, A. (1999). Compliance with treatment protocols: Interventions for children with chronic illness. *Archives of Disease in Children, 80,* 196–200.

Folkman, S., & Lazarus, R. S. (1988). The relationship between coping and emotion: Implications for theory and research. *Social Science and Medicine, 26,* 309–317.

Forero, R., Bauman, A., Young, L., Booth, M., & Nutbeam, D. (1996). Asthma, health behaviors, social adjustment, and psychosomatic symptoms in adolescence. *Journal of Asthma, 33,* 157–164.

Funck-Bretano, I., Dalban, C., Veber, F., Quartier, P., Hefez, S., Costagliola, D., & Blanche, S. (2005). Evaluation of a peer support group therapy for HIV-infected adolescents. *AIDS, 19,* 1501–1508.

Garralda, M. E. (1996). Somatisation in children. *Journal of Child Psychology and Psychiatry, 37,* 13–33.

Garralda, M. E., Jameson, R. A., Reynolds, J. M., & Postlethwaite, R. J. (1988). Psychiatric adjustment in children with chronic renal failure. *Journal of Child Psychology and Psychiatry, 29,* 79–90.

Garstein, M. A., Short, A. D., Vannatta, K. V., & Noll, R. B. (1999). Psychosocial adjustment of children with chronic illness: An evaluation of three models. *Developmental and Behavioral Pediatrics, 20,* 157–163.

Gil, K. M., Anthony, K. K., Carson, J, W., Redding-Lallinger, R., Daeschner, C. W., & Ware, R. E. (2001). Daily coping practice predicts treatment effects in children with sickle cell disease. *Journal of Pediatric Psychology, 26,* 163–173.

Gil, K. M., Porter, L., Ready, J., Workman, E., Sedway, J., & Anthony, K. K. (2000). Pain in children and adolescents with sickle cell disease: An analysis of daily pain diaries. *Children's Health Care, 29,* 225–241.

Gil, K. M., Williams, D. A., Thompson, R. J., & Kinney, T. R. (1991). Sickle cell disease in children and adolescents: The relation of child and parent pain coping strategies to adjustment. *Journal of Pediatric Psychology, 16,* 643–663.

Gill, L. J., Shand, P. A. X., Fuggle, P., Dugan, B., & Davies, S. C. (1997). Pain assessment for children with sickle cell disease: Improved validity of diary keeping versus interview ratings. *British Journal of Health Psychology, 2,* 131–140.

Glasscoe, C. A., & Quittner, A. L. (2003). Psychological interventions for cystic fibrosis. *Cochrane Database Systematic Review, 3,* CD003148.

Glazebrook, C., Hollis, C., Heussler, H., Goodman, R., & Coates, L. (2003). Detecting emotional and behavioural problems in paediatric clinics. *Child: Care, Health, and Development, 29,* 141–149.

Goldbeck, L., & Babka, C. (2001). Development and evaluation of a multi-family psychoeducational program for cystic fibrosis. *Patient Education and Counseling, 44,* 187–192.

Gortmaker, S. L., Walker, D. K., Weitzman, M., & Sobol, A. M. (1990). Chronic conditions, socioeconomic risks, and behavioral problems in children and adolescents. *Pediatrics, 85*, 267–276.

Gortmaker, S. L., & Sappenfield, W. (1984). Chronic childhood disorders: Prevalence and impact. *Pediatric Clinics of North America, 31*, 3–18.

Greco, P., Shroff-Pendley, J., McDonell, K., & Reeves, G. (2001). A peer group intervention for adolescents with type 1 diabetes and their best friends. *Journal of Pediatric Psychology, 8*, 485–490.

Greenberg, H. S., Kazak, A. E., & Meadows, A. T. (1989). Psychologic functioning in 8- to 16-year-old cancer survivors and their parents. *Journal of Pediatrics, 114*, 488–493.

Grey, M., Boland, E. A., Davidson, M., Li, J., & Tamborlane, W. V. (2000). Coping skills training for youth with diabetes mellitus has long-lasting effects on metabolic control and quality of life. *Journal of Pediatrics, 137*, 107–113.

Gustaffson, P. A., Kjellman, N., & Cederblad, M. (1986). Family therapy in the treatment of severe childhood asthma. *Journal of Psychosomatic Research, 30*, 369–374.

Hains, A. A., Davies, W. H., Behrens, D., & Biller, J. A. (1997). Cognitive behavioural interventions for adolescents with cystic fibrosis. *Journal of Pediatric Psychology, 22*, 669–687.

Hains, A. A., Davies, W. H., Behrens, D., Freeman, M. E., & Biller, J. A. (2001). Effectiveness of a cognitive behavioural intervention for young adults with cystic fibrosis. *Journal of Clinical Psychology in Medical Settings, 8*, 325–336.

Hains, A. A., Davies, W. H., Parton, E., & Silverman, A. H. (2001). A cognitive behavioral intervention for distressed adolescents with type 1 diabetes. *Journal of Pediatric Psychology, 26*, 61–66.

Hammen, C., & Rudolph, K. (1999). *UCLA life stress interview for children: Chronic stress and episodic life events.* Manual, University of Illinois.

Hanson, C. L. (1992). Developing systemic models of the adaptation of youths with diabetes. In A. M. La Greca, L. J. Siegel, J. L. Wallander, & C. E. Walker (Eds.), *Stress and coping in child health* (pp. 212–241). New York: Guilford Press.

Harbeck-Weber, C., Fisher, J. L., & Dittner, C. A. (2003). Promoting coping and enhancing adaptation to illness. In M. C. Roberts (Ed.), *Handbook of pediatric psychology* (3rd ed., pp. 99–118). New York: Guilford Press.

Harris, E. S., Canning, R. D., & Kelleher, K. J. (1996). A comparison of measures of adjustment, symptoms, and impairment among children with chronic medical conditions. *Journal of the American Academy of Child and Adolescent Psychiatry, 35*, 1025–1032.

Harris, M. A., Harris, B. S., & Mertlich, D. (2005). Brief report: In-home family therapy for adolescents with poorly controlled diabetes: Failure to maintain benefits at 6-month follow-up. *Journal of Pediatric Psychology, 30*, 683–688.

Haugaard, J. J. (2004). Recognizing and treating uncommon behavioral and emotional disorders in children and adolescents who have been severely maltreated: Somatization and other somatoform disorders. *Child Maltreatment, 9*, 169–176.

Henggeler, S. W., Schoenwald, S. K., Borduin, C. M., Rowland, M. D., & Cunningham, P. B. (1998). *Multisystemic treatment of antisocial behavior in children and adolescents.* New York: Guilford Press.

Hobbie, W. L., Stuber, M., Meeske, K., Wissler, K., Rourke, M. T., Ruccione, K., et al. (2000). Symptoms of posttraumatic stress in young adult survivors of childhood cancer. *Journal of Clinical Oncology, 18*, 4060–4066.

Hocking, M. C., & Lochman, J. E. (2005). Applying the transactional stress and coping model to sickle cell disorder and insulin-dependent diabetes mellitus: Identifying psychosocial variables related to adjustment and intervention. *Clinical Child and Family Psychology Review, 8*, 221–246.

Hodges, K., Kline, J., Stern, L., Cytryn, L., & McKnew, D. (1982). The development of a child assessment interview for research and clinical use. *Journal of Abnormal Child Psychology, 10*, 173–189.

Hoffman, L. (1981). *The foundations of family therapy.* New York: Basic Books.

Holden, G., Bearison, D. J., Rode, D. C., Kapiloff, M. F., & Rosenberg, G. (2000). The effects of a computer network on pediatric pain and anxiety. *Journal of Technology in Human Services, 17*, 27–47.

Holden, G., Bearison, D. J., Rode, D. C., Rosenberg, G., & Fishman, M. (1999). Evaluating the effects of a virtual environment (STARBRIGHT World) with hospitalized children. *Research on Social Work Practice, 9*, 365–382.

Holmes, C. S., Yu, Z., & Frentz, J. (1999). Chronic and discrete stress as predictors of children's adjustment. *Journal of Consulting and Clinical Psychology, 67*, 411–419.

Ievers, C. E., Brown, R. T., Lambert, R. G., Hsu, L., & Eckman, J. R. (1998). Family functioning and social support in the adaptation of caregivers of children with sickle cell syndromes. *Journal of Pediatric Psychology, 23*, 377–388.

Ingram, R. E., & Scott, W. D. (1990). Cognitive behavior therapy. In A. S. Bellack, M. Hersen, & A. E. Kazdin (Eds), *International handbook of behavior modification and therapy* (2nd ed., pp. 53–65). New York: Plenum Press.

Institute of Medicine. (1988). *Prenatal care: Reaching mothers, reaching infants.* Washington, DC: National Academy Press.

Isao, F., & Hiroko, K. (1995). Psychiatric problems of pediatric end-stage renal failure. *General Hospital Psychiatry, 17*, 32–36.

Jacobson, A. M., Hauser, S. T., Wertlieb, D., Woldsdorf, J., Orleans, J., & Viegra, M. (1986). Psychological adjustment of children with recently diagnosed diabetes mellitus. *Diabetes Care, 9*, 323–329.

Jellinek, M. S., Murphy, J. M., Little, M., Pagano, M. E., Comer, D. M., & Kelleher, K. J. (1999). Use of the pediatric symptom checklist to screen for psychosocial problems in pediatric primary care: A national feasibility study. *Archives of Pediatrics and Adolescent Medicine, 153*, 254–260.

Jerome, L., & Zaylor, C. (2000). Cyber-Space: Creating a therapeutic environment for telehealth applications. *Professional Psychology: Research and Practice, 31*, 478–483.

Johnson, K. B., Ravert, R. D., & Everton, A. (2001). Hopkins Teen Central: Assessment of an internet-based support system for children with cystic fibrosis. *Pediatrics, 107*, E24.

Jones, J. M., Lawson, M. L., Daneman, D., Olmsted, M. P., & Rodin, G. (2000). Eating disorders in adolescent females with and without type 1 diabetes: Cross sectional study. *British Medical Journal, 320*, 1563–1566.

Juniper, E. F, Guyatt, G. H, Feeny, D. H., Ferrie, P. J, Griffith, L. E., & Townsend, M. (1996). Measuring quality of life in children with asthma. *Quality of Life Research, 5*, 35–46.

Kaplan, H. I., Saddock, B. J., & Grebb, J. A. (1994). *Kaplan and Saddock's synopsis of psychiatry, behavioral sciences, clinical psychiatry.* Baltimore, MD: Williams & Wilkins.

Kaplan, R. M., Anderson, J. P., Wu, A. W., Mathews, W. C., Kozin, F., & Orenstein, D. (1989). The Quality of Well-Being Scale. *Medical Care, 27*, S27–S43.

Kaslow, K. J., Collins, M. H., Loundry, M. R., Brown, F., Hollins, L. D., & Eckman, J. (1997). Empirically validated family interventions for pediatric psychology: Sickle cell disease as an exemplar. *Journal of Pediatric Psychology, 22*, 213–227.

Kaslow, N. J., Tannenbaum, R. L., & Seligman, M. E. P. (1978). The KASTAN-R: A Children's Attributional Style Questionnaire (KASTAN-R CASQ). Unpublished manuscript. University of Pennsylvania, Philadelphia.

Katz, E. R., Rubinstein, C. L., Hubert, N. C., & Blew, A. (1988). School and social reintegration of children with cancer. *Journal of Psychosocial Oncology, 6*, 123–140.

Kazak, A. E., Alderfer, M., Rourke, M., Simms, S., Streisand, R., & Grossman, J. (2004). Posttraumatic stress symptoms (PTSS) and posttraumatic stress disorder in families of adolescent childhood cancer survivors. *Journal of Pediatric Psychology, 29*, 211–219.

Kazak, A., Alderfer, M., Streisand, R., Simms, S., Rourke, M., Barakat, L., et al. (2004). Treatment of posttraumatic stress symptoms in adolescent survivors of childhood cancer and their families: A randomized clinical trial. *Journal of Family Psychology, 18*, 493–504.

Kazak, A., Barakat, L., Alderfer, M., Rourke, M., Meeske, K., Gallagher, P., et al. (2001). Posttraumatic stress in survivors of childhood cancer and mothers: Development and validation of the Impact of Traumatic Stressors Interview Schedule (ITSIS). *Journal of Clinical Psychology in Medical Settings, 8*, 307–323.

Kazak, A., Cant, M. C., Jensen, M., McSherry, M., Rourke, M., Hwang, W. T., et al. (2003). Identifying psychosocial risk indicative of subsequent resource utilization in families of newly diagnosed pediatric oncology patients. *Journal of Clinical Oncology, 21*, 3220–3225.

Kazak, A. E., Penati, B., Boyer, B. A., Himelstein, B., Brophy, P., Waibel, M. K., et al., (1996). A randomized controlled prospective outcome study of a psychological and pharmacological intervention protocol for procedural distress in pediatric leukemia. *Journal of Pediatric Psychology, 21*, 615–631.

Kazak, A., Prusak, A., McSherry, M., Simms, S., Beele, D., Rourke, M., et al. (2001). The Psychosocial Assessment Tool (PAT): Pilot data on a brief screening instrument for identifying high risk families in pediatric oncology. *Families Systems and Health, 19*, 303–317.

Kazdin, A. E., & Nock, M. K. (2003). Delineating mechanisms of change in child and adolescent therapy: Methodological issues and research recommendations. *Journal of Child Psychology and Psychiatry, 44*, 1116–1129.

Kendall, P. C. (2000). Guiding theory for therapy with children and adolescents. In P. C. Kendall (Ed.), *Child and adolescent therapy: Cognitive-behavioral procedures* (2nd ed., pp. 3–27). New York: Guilford Press.

Key, J. D., Brown, R. T., Marsh, L. D., Spratt, E. J., & Recknor, J. C. (2001). Depressive symptoms in adolescents with a chronic illness. *Children's Health Care, 30*, 283–292.

Kibby, M. Y., Tyc, V. L., & Mulhern, R. K. (1998). Effectiveness of psychological intervention for children and adolescents with chronic medical illness: A meta-analysis. *Clinical Psychology Review, 18*, 103–117.

Klinnert, M. D., McQuaid, E. L., McCormick, D., Adinoff, A. D., & Bryant, N. E. (2000). A multimethod assessment of behavioral and emotional adjustment in children with asthma. *Journal of Pediatric Psychology, 25*, 35–46.

Koocher, G. P., McGrath, M. L., & Gudas, L. J. (1990). Typologies of nonadherence in cystic fibrosis. *Developmental and Behavioral Pediatrics, 11*, 353–358.

Kovacs, M. (1992). Children's Depression Inventory (CDI) manual. North Tonawanda, NY: Multi-Health Systems.

Kupst, M. J. (1999). Assessment of psychoeducational and emotional functioning. In R. T. Brown (Ed.), *Cognitive aspects of chronic illness in children* (pp. 25–46). New York: Guilford.

La Greca, A. M., & Bearman, K. J. (2003). Adherence to pediatric regimens. In M. C. Roberts (Ed.), *Handbook of pediatric psychology* (3rd ed., pp. 119–140). New York: Guilford.

La Greca, A. M., Follansbee, D., & Skyler, J. S. (1990). Developmental and behavioral aspects of diabetes management in youngsters. *Children's Health Care, 19*, 132–139.

Landgraf, J. M., Abetz, L., & Ware, J. E. (1996). *The CHQ user's manual* (1st ed.). Boston, MA: The Health Institute, New England Medical Center.

Larcombe, I. J., Walker, J., Charlton, R., Meller, S., Jones, P. M., & Mott, M. G. (1991). Implications of childhood cancer on return to normal schooling. *Medical Journal, 301*, 169–175.

Lavigne, J. V., & Faier-Routman, J. (1992). Psychological adjustment to pediatric physical disorders: A meta-analytic review. *Journal of Pediatric Psychology, 17*, 133–157.

LeBovidge, J. S., Lavigne, J.V., & Miller, M. L. (2005). Adjustment to chronic arthritis of childhood: The roles of illness-related stress and attitude toward illness. *Journal of Pediatric Psychology, 30*, 273–286.

Lemanek, K. L., Kamps, J., & Chung, N. B. (2001). Empirically supported treatments in pediatric psychology: Regimen adherence. *Journal of Pediatric Psychology, 26*, 253–275.

Lemanek, K. L., Ranalli, M. A., Green, K., Biega, C., & Lupia, C. (2003). Diseases of the blood. Sickle cell disease and hemophilia. In M. C. Roberts (Ed.), *Handbook of Pediatric Psychology* (3rd ed., pp. 321–340). New York: Guildford.

Levitan, I. B. (1989). The basic defect in cystic fibrosis. *Science, 244*, 1423.

Lewis, H. A., & Kliewer, W. (1996). Hope, coping, and adjustment among children with sickle cell disease: Tests of mediator and moderator models. *Journal of Pediatric Psychology, 21*, 25–41.

Lewiston, N. J. (1985). Cystic fibrosis. In N. Hobbs & J. M. Perrin (Eds.), *Issues in the care of children with chronic illness* (pp. 196–213). San Francisco: Jossey-Bass.

Limb, S., Brown, K., Wood, R., Wise, R., Eggleston, P., Tonascia, J., et al. (2005). Adult asthma severity in individuals with a history of childhood asthma. *Journal of Allergy and Clinical Immunology, 115*, 61–66.

Martiniuk, A. (2003). Camping programs for children with cancer and their families. *Support Care Cancer, 11*, 749–757.

McConaughy, S. H., & Achenbach, T. M. (1994). Comorbidity of empirically matched syndromes in matched general population and clinical samples. *Journal of Child Psychology and Psychiatry, 35*, 1141–1157.

McCormick, M. C. (1985). The contribution of low birth weight to infant mortality and childhood morbidity. *New England Journal of Medicine, 312*, 82–90.

McDaniel, S. H., Hepworth, J., & Doherty, W. (1992). *Medical family therapy: A biopsychosocial approach to families with health problems*. New York: Basic Books.

McQuaid, E. L., Kopel, S. J., Klein, R. B., & Fritz, G. K. (2003). Medication adherence in pediatric asthma: Reasoning, responsibility, and behavior. *Journal of Pediatric Psychology, 28*, 3232–3333.

McQuaid, E. L., Kopel, S. J., & Nassau, J. H. (2001). Behavioral adjustment in children with asthma: A meta-analysis. *Journal of Developmental and Behavioral Pediatrics, 22*, 430–439.

McQuaid, E. L., & Nassau, J. H. (1999). Empirically supported treatments in pediatric psychology: Asthma, diabetes, and cancer. *Journal of Pediatric Psychology, 24*, 305–328.

McQuaid, E. L., & Walders, N. (2003). Pediatric asthma. In M. C. Roberts (Ed.), *Handbook of pediatric psychology* (3rd ed., pp. 269–285). New York: The Guildford Press.

Meichenbaum, D. C., & Turk, D. (1987). *Facilitating treatment adherence: A practitioner's guidebook*. New York: Plenum Press.

Meijer, S. A., Sinnema, G., Bijstra, J. O., Mellenbergh, G. J., & Wolters, W. H. (2000a). Peer interaction in adolescents with a chronic illness. *Personality and Individual Differences, 29*, 799–813.

Meijer, S. A., Sinnema, G., Bijstra, J. O., Mellenbergh, G. J., & Wolters, W. H. (2000b). Social functioning in children with a chronic illness. *Journal of Child Psychology and Psychiatry, 41*, 309–317.

Meijer, S. A., Sinnema, G., Bijstra, J. O., Mellenbergh, G. J., & Wolters, W. H. G. (2002). Coping styles and locus of control as predictors for psychological adjustment of adolescent with a chronic illness. *Social Science Medicine, 54*, 1453–1461.

Miller, J. E. (2000). The effects of race/ethnicity and income on early childhood asthma prevalence and health care issues. *American Journal of Public Health, 90*, 428–430.

Merrick, J., & Carmeli, E. (2003). A review on the prevalence of disabilities in children. *Internet Journal of Pediatrics and Neonatology, 3*(1). Retrieved February 7, 2006, from http://www.ispub.com/ostia/index.php?xmlFilePath=journals/ijpn/vol3n1/prevalence.xml.

Minuchin, S., Montalvo, B., Guerney, B., Rosman, B., & Schumer, F. (1967). *Families of the slums: An exploration of their structure and treatment*. New York: Basic Books.

Modi, A. C., Lim, C. S., Yu, N., Geller, D., Wagner, M. H., & Quittner, A. L. (2006). A multi-method assessment of treatment adherence for children with cystic fibrosis. *Journal of Cystic Fibrosis, 5*, 177–185.

Modi, A. C., & Quittner, A. L. (2003). Validation of a disease-specific measure of health-related quality of life for children with cystic fibrosis. *Journal of Pediatric Psychology, 28*, 535–546.

Modi, A. C., & Quittner, A. L. (2006). Barriers to treatment adherence for children with cystic fibrosis and asthma: What gets in the way? *Journal of Pediatric Psychology, 31*, 846–858.

Moons, P., Barrea, C., Suys, B., Ovaert, C., Boshoff, D., Eyskens, B., et al. (2006). Improved perceived health status persists three months after a special sports camp for children with congenital heart disease. *European Journal of Pediatrics, 165*, 767–772.

Moos, R. H., & Moos, B. S. (1991). Family environment scale manual. Palo Alto, CA: Consulting Psychologists Press.

Morgan, S. A., & Jackson, J. (1986). Psychological and social concomitants of sickle cell anemia in adolescents. *Journal of Pediatric Psychology, 11*, 429–440.

Mortweet, S. L., & Christophersen, E. R. (2003). Behavior problems in a pediatric context. In M. C. Roberts (Ed.), *Handbook of Pediatric Psychology* (3rd ed., pp. 599–616). New York: Guildford.

Mulhern, R. K., & Butler, R. T. (2004). Neurocognitive sequelae of childhood cancers and their treatment. *Pediatric Rehabilitation, 7*, 1–14.

Nassau, J., & Drotar, D. (1995). Social competence in children with IDDM and asthma: Child, teacher, and parent reports of children's social adjustment, social performance, and social skills. *Journal of Pediatric Psychology, 20*, 187–204.

National Healthcare Quality/Disparities Report. (2004). *Selected Findings on Child and Adolescent Health Care from the 2004 National Healthcare Quality/Disparities Reports*. Fact Sheet. AHRQ Publication No. 05-P011, March 2005. Agency for Healthcare Research and Quality, Rockville, MD. Available at http://www.ahrq.gov/qual/nhqrchild/nhqrchild.htm.

National Heart, Lung, and Blood Institute. (1996). *Facts about sickle cell anemia* (Publication no. 96–4057). Bethesda, MD: National Institutes of Health.

National Institutes of Health (NHIS). (1997). *National Asthma Education and Prevention Program (National Heart, Lung, and Blood Institute) Second Expert Panel on the Management of Asthma. Expert Panel Report 2: Guidelines for the diagnosis and management of asthma* (DHHS Publication No. 95–3675). Bethesda, MA: Author.

Newacheck, P. W. (1994). Poverty and childhood chronic illness. *Archive of Pediatric Adolescent Medicine, 148*, 1143–1149.

Newacheck, P. W., & Stoddard, J. (1994). Prevalence and impact of multiple childhood chronic illnesses. *Journal of Pediatrics, 124*, 40–48.

Newacheck, P. W., Strickland, J. P., Shonkoff, J. M., Perrin, M., McPherson, M., McManus, C. et al. (1998). An epidemiologic profile of children with special health care needs. *Pediatrics, 102*, 117–123.

Newacheck, P. W., & Taylor, W. R. (1992). Childhood chronic illness: Prevalence, severity, and impact. *American Journal of Public Health, 82*, 364–371.

Noll, R. B., Gartstein, M., Vannatta, K., Correll, J., Bukowski, W., & Davies, H. W. (1999). Social, emotional, and behavioral functioning of children with cancer. *Pediatrics, 103*, 71–92.

Noll, R. B., Ris, M. D., Davies, W. H., Bukowski, W. M., & Koontz, K. (1992). Social interactions between children with cancer or sickle cell disease and their peers: Teacher ratings. *Journal of Developmental and Behavioral Pediatrics, 13*, 187–193.

Olson, A. L., Johansen, S. G., Powers, L. E., Pope, J. B., & Klein, R. B. (1993). Cognitive coping strategies of children with chronic illness. *Journal of Developmental and Behavior Pediatrics, 14*, 217–223.

Olson, D. H. (1986). Circumplex Model VII: Validation studies and FACES III. *Family Process, 25*, 337–351.

Olsson, C. A., Boyce, M. F., Toumbourou, J. W., & Sawyer, S. S. (2005). The role of peer support in facilitating psychosocial adjustment to chronic illness in adolescence. *Clinical Child Psychiatry and Psychology, 10*, 78–87.

Olsson, C. A., Sawyer, S. S., & Boyce, M. F. (2000). What are the special needs of chronically ill young people? *Australian Family Physician, 29*, 1–2.

Olsson, C. A., & Toumbourou, J. W. (1996). Chronic illness peer support: Assisting young people adjust to life with a chronic illness. In J. Izard & J. Evans (Eds.), *Student behaviour: Policies, interventions, and evaluations* (pp. 257–267). Melbourne: The Australian Council for Educational Research.

Olsson, C. A., Walsh, B., Toumbourou, J. W., & Bowes, G. (1997). Chronic illness peer support. *Australian Family Physician, 26*, 500–501.

Ortega, A. N., Huertas, S. E., Canino, G., Ramirez, R., & Rubio-Stipec, M. (2002). Childhood asthma, chronic illness, and psychiatric disorders. *Journal of Nervous and Mental Disease, 190*, 275–281.

Parcel, G., & Meyer, M. (1978). Development of an instrument to measure children's health locus of control. *Health Education Monographs, 6*, 149–159.

Partridge A. H., Avorn J., Wang P. S., & Winer E. P. (2002). Adherence to therapy with oral antoneoplastic agents. *Journal of the National Cancer Institute, 94*, 652–661.

Penza-Clyve, S., McQuaid, E. L., & Mansell, C. (2004). Why don't children take their asthma medications? Results from focus group data. *Journal of Asthma, 41*, 131–139.

Perrin, E. C., Newacheck, P. W., & Pless, I. B. (1993). Issues involved in the definition and classification of chronic health conditions. *Pediatrics, 91*, 787–793.

Perrin, E. C., Stein, R. E. K., & Drotar, D. (1991). Cautions on using the Child Behavior Checklist: Observations based on research about children with a chronic illness. *Journal of Pediatric Psychology, 16*, 411–421.

Perrin, J. M., & MacLean, W. E. Jr. (1988). Children with chronic illness: The prevention of dysfunction. *Pediatric Clinics of North America, 35*, 1325–1337.

Perrin, J. M., MacLean, W. E., Jr., Gortmaker, S. L., & Asher, K. N. (1992). Improving the psychological status of children with asthma: A randomized controlled trial. *Journal of Developmental and Behavioral Pediatrics, 13*, 241–247.

Plante, W., Lobato, D., & Engel, R. (2001). Review of group interventions for pediatric chronic conditions. *Journal of Pediatric Psychology, 26*, 435–453.

Powers, S. (1999). Empirically supported treatments in pediatric psychology: Procedure-related pain. *Journal of Pediatric Psychology, 24*, 131–145.

Pumariega, A. J., Pearson, D. A., & Seilheimer, D. K. (1993). Family and childhood adjustment in cystic fibrosis. *Journal of Child and Family Studies, 2*, 109–118.

Quinn, C. T., Rogers, Z. R., & Buchanan, G. R. (2004). Survival of children with sickle cell disease. *Blood, 103*, 4023–4027.

Quittner, A. L., & DiGirolamo, A. M. (1998). Family adaptation to childhood disability and illness. In R. T. Ammerman & J. V. Campo (Eds.), *Handbook of pediatric psychology and psychiatry: Vol. 2* (pp. 70–102). Boston: Allyn & Bacon.

Quittner, A. L., Drotar, D., Ievers-Landis, C., & De Lambo, K. (2004, August). *Changing adolescent adherence behaviors: The role of family relationships.* Paper presented at the 112th Annual Convention of the American Psychological Association, Honolulu, HI.

Quittner, A. L., Drotar, D., Ievers-Landis, C., Seidner, D., Slocum, N., & Jacobsen, J. (2000). Adherence to medical treatments in adolescents with cystic fibrosis: The development and evaluation of family-based interventions. In D. Drotar (Ed.), *Promoting adherence to medical treatment in childhood chronic illness: Concepts, Methods, and Interventions* (pp.383–407). Mahwah NJ: Lawrence Erlbaum Associates.

Radcliffe, J., Bennett, D., Kazak, A. E., Foley, B., & Phillips, P. (1996). Adjustment in childhood brain tumor survival: Child, mother, and teacher. *Journal of Pediatric Psychology, 21*, 529–539.

Rapoff, M. A., & Barnard, M. U. (1991). Compliance with pediatric medical regimens. In J. A. Cramer & B. Spiker (Eds.), *Patient compliance in medical practice and clinical trials* (pp. 73–98). New York: Raven.

Reiter-Purtill, J., & Noll, R. B. (2003). Peer relationships of children with chronic illness. In M. C. Roberts (Ed.), *Handbook of pediatric psychology* (3rd ed., pp. 176–197). New York: Guilford Press.

Reynolds, C. R., & Kamphaus, R. W. (1992). *The behavior assessment system for children.* Circle Pines, MN: American Guidance Service (AGS), Inc.

Reynolds, C. R., & Richmond, B. O. (1978). What I think and feel: A revised measure of children's manifest anxiety. *Journal of Abnormal Psychology, 6*, 271–280.

Richardson, J., Smith, J. E., McCall, G., & Pilkington, J. (2006). Hypnosis for procedure-related pain and distress in pediatric cancer patients: A systematic review of effectiveness and methodology related to hypnosis interventions. *Journal of Pain and Symptom Management, 31*, 70–84.

Robin, A., & Foster, S. L. (1989). *Negotiating parent adolescent conflict.* New York: Guilford Press.

Roid, G. H. (2003). *Stanford-Binet Intelligence Scales, Fifth Edition, Technical Manual.* Itasca, IL: Riverside.

Rolland, J. S. (1987). Chronic illness and the life cycle: A conceptual framework. *Family Process, 26,* 203–221.

Rourke, M., Hobbie, W., & Kazak, A. (2002). *Posttraumatic stress in young adult survivors of childhood cancer.* Paper presented at the 7th International Conference on long-term complications of treatment of children and adolescents for cancer, Niagara on the lake, Ontario, Canada.

Rutter, M. (1988). Epidemiological approaches to developmental psychopathology. *Archives of General Psychiatry, 45,* 486–495.

Sabbeth, B., & Stein, R. E. (1990). Mental health referral: A weak link in comprehensive care of children with chronic physical illness. *Journal of Developmental and Behavioral Pediatrics, 11,* 73–78.

Sandler, I. N., Tein, J. Y., & West, S. G. (1994). Coping, stress, and the psychological symptoms of children of divorce: A cross-sectional and longitudinal study. Child Development, *65,* 1744–1763.

Sargent, J. (1983). The sick child: Family complications. *Journal of Developmental and Behavioral Pediatrics, 4,* 50–56.

Satin, W., La Greca, A. M., Zigo, S., & Skyler, J. S. (1989). Diabetes in adolescence: Effects of multifamily group intervention and parent simulation of diabetes. *Journal of Pediatric Psychology, 14,* 259–276.

Sawyer, M., Antoniou, G., Toogood, I., & Rice, M. (1997). Childhood cancer: A two-year prospective study of the psychological adjustment of children and parents. *Journal of the American Academy of Child and Adolescent Psychiatry, 36,* 1736–1743.

Schwartz, C. E., Feinberg, R. G., Jilinskala, E., & Applegate, J. C. (1999). An evaluation of a psychosocial intervention for survivors of childhood cancer: Paradoxical effects of response shift over time. *Psycho-Oncology, 8,* 344–354.

Seiffge-Krenke, I. (2001). *Diabetic adolescents and their families: Stress, coping, and adaptation.* New York: Cambridge University Press.

Sexson, S. B., & Madan-Swain, A. (1993). School reentry for the child with chronic illness. *Journal of Learning Disabilities, 26,* 115–125.

Shaffer, D., Fisher, P., Lucas, C. P., Dulcan, M. K., & Schwab-Stone, M. H. (2000). NIMH Diagnostic Interview Schedule for Children Version IV (NIMH DISC-IV): Description, differences from previous versions, and reliability of some common diagnoses. *Journal of the American Academy of Child and Adolescent Psychiatry, 39,* 28–38.

Sharpe, D., & Rossiter, L. (2002). Siblings of children with a chronic illness: A meta-analysis. *Journal of Pediatric Psychology, 27,* 699–710.

Shemesh, E., Yehuda, R., Rockmore, L., Shneider, B. L., Emre, S., Bartell, A. S., et al. (2005). Assessment of depression in medically ill children presenting to pediatric specialty clinics. *Journal of the American Academy of Child and Adolescent Psychiatry, 44,* 1249–1257.

Shepanski, M. A., Hurd, L. B., Culton, K., Markowitz, J. E., Mamula, P., & Baldassano, R. N. (2005). Health-related quality of life improves in children and adolescents with inflammatory bowel disease after attending a camp sponsored by the Crohn's and Colitis Foundation of America. *Inflammatory Bowel Diseases, 11,* 164–170.

Sifers, S. K., Puddy, R. W., Warren, J. S., & Roberts, M. C. (2002). Reporting of demographics, methodology, and ethical procedures in journals in pediatric and child psychology. *Journal of Pediatric Psychology, 27,* 19–25.

Simmons, R. J., & Goldberg, S. (2001). Infants and pre-school children. In M. Bluebond-Langner, B. Lask, & D. B. Angst (Eds.), *Psychosocial aspects of cystic fibrosis* (pp. 110-124). New York: Oxford University Press.

Soliday, E., Kool, E., & Lande, M. B. (2000). Psychosocial adjustment in children with kidney disease. *Journal of Pediatric Psychology, 25,* 93–103.

Spielberger, C. D., Edwards, C. D., Lushene, R. E., Monuori, J., & Platzek, D. (1973). *STAIC manual: State-Trait Anxiety Inventory for Children.* Palo Alto, CA: Consulting Psychologist Press.

Spirito, A., DeLawyer, D. D., & Stark, L. J. (1991). Peer relations and social adjustment of chronically ill children and adolescents. *Clinical Psychology Review, 11,* 539–564.

Spirito, A., & Kazak, A. (2006). *Effective and emerging treatments in pediatric psychology.* New York: Oxford University Press.

Spirito, A., Stark, L. J., & Williams, C. (1988). Development of a brief coping checklist for use with pediatric populations. *Journal of Pediatric Psychology, 13,* 555–574.

Stark, L. J., Opipari, L. C., Spieth, L. E., Jelalian, E., Quittner, A. L., Higgins, L., et al. (2003). Contribution of behavior therapy to dietary treatment in cystic fibrosis: A randomized controlled study with two-year follow-up. *Behavior Therapy, 34,* 237–258.

Stein, R. E., & Jessop, D. J. (1982). A noncategorical approach to chronic childhood illness. *Public Health Reports, 97,* 354–362.

Stein, R. E., & Jessop, D. J. (1989). What diagnosis does not tell: The case for a noncategorical approach to chronic illness in childhood. *Social Science and Medicine, 29,* 769–778.

Stein, R. E., & Jessop, D. J. (1990). *Manual for personal adjustment and role skills scale III (PARS III).* Pacts Papers, Albert Einstein College of Medicine of Yeshiva University.

Stein, R. E., & Jessop, D. J. (2003). The impact on family scale revisited: Further psychometric data. *Journal of Developmental and Behavioral Pediatrics, 24,* 9–16.

Stein, R. E., & Riessman, C. K. (1980). The development of an Impact-On-Family Scale: Preliminary findings. *Medical Care, 18,* 465–472.

Stein, R. E., & Silver, E. J. (1999). Operationalizing a conceptually based noncategorical definition. A first look at U.S. children with chronic conditions. *Archives of Pediatric and Adolescent Medicine, 153,* 68–74.

Stone, M. H., Jastak, S., & Wilkinson, G. (1995). Wide Range Achievement Test – Third Edition (WRAT-3). Wilmington, DE: Wide Range.

Sue, D., Sue, D., & Sue, S. (1994). *Understanding abnormal behavior.* Boston: Houghton Mifflin.

Suris, J. (1995). Global trends of young people with chronic and disabling condition. *Journal of Adolescent Health, 17,* 17–22.

Suris, J. C., Michaud, P. A., & Viner, R. (2004). The adolescent with a chronic condition. Part I: Developmental issues. *Archives of Disease in Childhood, 89,* 938–942.

Tarnowski, K. T., Brown, R. T., & Simonian, S. J. (1999). Social class. In W. Silverman & T. Ollendick (Eds.), *Developmental issues in the clinical treatment of children* (pp. 213–230). Boston: Allyn & Bacon.

Taylor, W. R., & Newacheck, P. W. (1992). Impact of childhood asthma on health. *Pediatrics, 90,* 657–662.

Taylor, L., Simpson, K., Bushardt, R., Reeves, C., Elkin, D., Fortson, B., et al. (2006). Insurance barriers for childhood survivors of pediatric brain tumors: The case for neurocognitive evaluations. *Pediatric Neurosurgery, 42,* 223–227.

The Psychological Corporation. (2001). WIAT–II Examiner's Manual. San Antonio, TX: Author.

Thompson, R. J. Jr., Armstrong, F. D., Link, C. L., Pegelow, C. H., Moser, F., Wang, W. C. (2003). A prospective study of the relationship over time of behavior problems, intellectual functioning, and family functioning in children with sickle cell disease: A report from the cooperative study of sickle cell disease. *Journal of Pediatric Psychology, 28,* 59–65.

Thompson, R. J. Jr., Gil, K., Burbach, D., Keith, B., & Kinney, T. (1993). Role of child and maternal processes in the psychological adjustment of children with sickle cell disease. *Journal of Consulting and Clinical Psychology, 61,* 468–474.

Thompson, R. J. Jr., & Gustafson, K. E. (1996). *Adaptation to chronic childhood illness.* Washington, DC: American Psychological Association.

Thompson, R. J. Jr., Gustafson, K. E., George, L. K., & Spock, A. (1994). Change over a 12-month period in the psychological adjustment of children and adolescents with cystic fibrosis. *Journal of Pediatric Psychology, 19,* 189–203.

Thompson, R. J. Jr., Gustafson, K. E., Gil, K. M., Godfrey, J., & Bennett-Murphy, L. M. (1998). Illness specific patterns of psychological adjustment and cognitive adaptational processes in children with cystic fibrosis and sickle cell disease. *Journal of Clinical Psychology, 54*, 121–128.

Thompson, R. J. Jr., Gustafson, K. E., Gil, K. M., Kinney, T. R., & Spock, A. (1999). Change in the psychological adjustment of children with cystic fibrosis or sickle cell disease and their mothers. *Journal of Clinical Psychology in the Medical Settings, 6*, 373–392.

Thompson, R. J. Jr., Gustafson, K. E., Hamlett, K. W., & Spock, A. (1992). Stress, coping, and family functioning in the psychological adjustment of mothers of children and adolescents with cystic fibrosis. *Journal of Pediatric Psychology, 17*, 573–585.

Timko, C., Stovel, K. W., Baumgartner, M., & Moos, R. H. (1995). Acute and chronic stressors, social resources, and functioning among adolescents with juvenile rheumatic disease. *Journal of Research on Adolescence, 5*, 361–385.

Tobin, D. L., Holroyd, K. A., & Reynolds, R. V. (1989). The hierarchical factor structure of the coping strategies inventory. *Coping Theory and Research, 13*, 343–361.

Treadwell, M., Law, A. W., Sung, J., Hackney-Stephens, E., Quirolo, K., Murray, E., et al. (2005). Barriers to adherence of deferoxamine usage in sickle cell disease. *Pediatric Blood and Cancer, 44*, 1–8.

van Dyck, P. C., Kogan, M. D., McPherson, M. G., Weissman, G. R., & Newacheck, P. W. (2004). Prevalence and characteristics of children with special health care needs. *Archives of Pediatric and Adolescent Medicine, 158*, 884–990.

van Schoor, E. P., Schmidt, K., & Ghuman, H. S. (1998). Group psychotherapy with children and adolescents: Key issues. In H. S. Ghuman & R. M. Sarles (Eds.), *Handbook of child and adolescent outpatient, day treatment and community psychiatry* (pp. 283–297). Levittown, PA: Brunner/Mazel.

Varni, J. W., Katz, E. R., Colegrove, R., & Dolgin, M. (1993). The impact of social skills training on the adjustment of children with newly diagnosed cancer. *Journal of Pediatric Psychology, 18*, 751–767.

Varni, J. W., Katz, E. R., Colegrove, R., & Dolgin, M. (1994). Perceived social support and adjustment of children with newly diagnosed cancer. *Journal of Developmental and Behavioral Pediatrics, 15*, 20–26.

Varni, J. W., Katz, E. R., Colegrove, R., & Dolgin, M. (1995). Perceived physical appearance and adjustment of children with newly diagnosed cancer: A path analytic model. *Journal of Behavioral Medicine, 18*, 261–278.

Varni, J. W., Katz, E. R., Seid, M., Quiggins, D. J. L., & Friedman-Bender, A. (1998). The Pediatric Cancer Quality of Life Inventory-32 (PCQL-32): I. Reliability and validity. *Cancer, 82*, 1184–1196.

Varni, J. W., Setoguchi, Y., Rappaport, L. T., & Talbot, D. (1991). Effects of stress, social support, and self-esteem on depression in children with limb deficiencies. *Archives of Physical Medicine and Rehabilitation, 72*, 1053–1058.

Velsor-Friedrich, B., Pigott, T., & Srof, B. (2005). A practitioner-based asthma intervention with African-American inner-city school children. *Journal of Pediatric Health Care, 19*, 163–171.

von Weiss, R. T., Rapoff, M. A., Varni, J. W., Lindsley, C. B., Olson, N. Y., Madson, K. L., et al. (2002). Daily hassles and social support as predictors of adjustment in children with pediatric rheumatic disease. *Journal of Pediatric Psychology, 27*, 155–165.

Wagener, J. S., Sontag, M. K., Sagel, S. D., & Accurso, F. J. (2004). Update on newborn screening for cystic fibrosis. *Current Opinion in Pulmonary Medicine, 10*, 500–504.

Walders, N., Kercsmar, C., Schluchter, M., Redline, S., Kirchner, H. L., & Drotar, D. (2006). An interdisciplinary intervention for undertreated pediatric asthma. *Chest, 129*, 292–299.

Wallander, J. L., & Thompson, R. J., Jr. (1995). Psychosocial adjustment of children with chronic physical conditions. In M. C. Roberts (Ed.), *Handbook of pediatric psychology* (2nd ed., pp. 124–141). New York: Guilford.

Wallander, J. L., Thompson, R. J., & Alriksson-Smith, A. (2003). Psychosocial adjustment of children with chronic physical conditions. In M. C. Roberts (Ed.), *Handbook of Pediatric Psychology* (3rd ed., pp. 141–158). New York: Guildford.

Wallander, J. L., & Varni, J. W. (1998). Effects of pediatric chronic physical disorders on child and family adjustment. *Journal of Child Psychology and Psychiatry, 39*, 29–46.

Wallander, J. L., Varni, J. W., Babani, L., Banis, H. T., & Wilcox, K. T. (1989). Family resources as resistance factors for psychological maladjustment in chronically ill and handicapped children. *Journal of Pediatric Psychology, 14*, 157–173.

Wamboldt, M. Z., Fritz, G., Mansell, A., McQuaid, E. L., & Klein, R. B. (1998). Relationship of asthma severity and psychological problems in children. *Journal of the American Academy of Child and Adolescent Psychiatry, 37*, 943–950.

Wechsler, D. (2002). *Wechsler Preschool and Primary Scales of Intelligence – Third Edition.* San Antonio, TX: The Psychological Corporation.

Wechsler, D. (2003). *Wechsler Intelligence Scales for Children – Fourth Edition.* San Antonio, TX: The Psychological Corporation.

Weersing, V. R., & Weisz, J. R. (2002). Mechanisms of action in youth psychotherapy. *Journal of Child Psychology and Psychiatry, 43*, 3–29.

Weiland, S. K, Pless, I. B., & Roghmann, K. J. (1992). Chronic illness and mental health problems in pediatric practice: Results from a survey of primary care providers. *Pediatrics, 89*, 445–449.

Weiss, K. (1996). Introduction to the supplement of: National asthma education and prevention program task force report on the cost effectiveness, quality of care, and financing of asthma care. *Respiratory and Critical Care Medicine, 154*, 582–583.

Weist, M. D., & Danforth, J. S. (1998). Cognitive-behavioral therapy with children and adolescents. In H. Ghuman & R. Sarles (Eds.), *Handbook of child and adolescent outpatient, day treatment, and community psychiatry* (pp. 235–244). New York: Bruner/Mazel.

Weitzman, M. (1986). School absence rates as outcome measures in studies of children with chronic illness. *Journal of Chronic Disease, 39*, 799–808.

Westbrook, L., & Stein, R. (1994). Epidemiology of chronic health conditions in adolescents. *Adolescent Medicine State of the Art Reviews, 5*, 197–209.

Wilson, J., Fosson, A., Kanga, J. F., & D'Angelo, S. L. (1996). Homeostatic interactions: A longitudinal study of biological, psychosocial, and family variables in children with cystic fibrosis. *Journal of Family Therapy, 18*, 123–139.

Winkley, K., Landau, S., Eisler, I., & Ismail, K. (2006). Psychological interventions to improve glycaemic control in patients with type 1 diabetes: Systematic review and meta-analysis of randomised controlled trials. *British Medical Journal, 333*, 65.

Wise, P. H. (2004). The transformation of child health in the United States: Social disparities in child health persistent despite dramatic improvement in child health overall. *Health Affairs, 23*, 9–25.

Wolf, F. M., Guevara, J. P., Grum, C. M., Clark, N. M., & Cates, C. J. (2003). Educational interventions for asthma in children. *Cochrane Database Systematic Reviews, 1*, CD000326.

Woodcock, R. W., McGrew, K. S., & Mather, N. (2001). Woodcock-Johnson III Tests of Achievement. Itasca, IL: Riverside.

Wysocki, T. (2006). Behavioral assessment and intervention in pediatric diabetes. *Behavioral Modification, 30*, 72–92.

Wysocki, T., Greco, P., & Buckloh, L. M. (2003). Childhood diabetes in psychological context. In M. C. Roberts (Ed.), *Handbook of Pediatric Psychology* (3rd ed., pp. 304–320). New York: Guildford.

Wysocki, T., Greco, P., Harris, M. A., Bubb, J., & White, N. H. (2001). Behavior therapy for families of adolescents with IDDM: Maintenance of treatment effects. *Diabetes Care, 24*, 441–446.

Wysocki, T., Green, L., & Huxtable, K. (1989). Blood glucose monitoring by diabetic adolescents: Compliance and metabolic control. *Health Psychology, 8*, 267–284.

Young, G. A. (1994). Asthma: Medical issues. In R. A. Olson, L. L. Mullins, J. B. Gillman, & J. M. Chaney (Eds.), *The sourcebook of pediatric psychology* (pp. 57–60). Boston: Allyn & Bacon.

Zeiger, R. S., Dawson, C., & Weiss, S. (1999). Relationship between duration of asthma and asthma severity among children in the Childhood Asthma Management Program. *Journal of Allergy and Clinical Immunology, 103*, 376–387.

8

Appendix: Tools and Resources

Pediatric Chronic Illness
Starlight-Starbright Children's Foundation
5757 Wilshire Blvd. Suite M100
Los Angeles, CA 90036
Tel.: +1 310-479-1212
Web site: http://www.starlight.org
Excellent site that details programs that educate, entertain, and inspire seriously ill children.

Asthma
Bender, B. *Childhood asthma*. Washington, DC: American Psychological Association.
APA Service Center
750 First Street, NE
Washington, DC 20002-4242
Tel.: +1 202-336-5510 or 800-374-2721
TDD/TTY: 202-336-6123
Fax: +1 202-336-5502
This video is part of the Behavioral Health and Health Counseling APA Psychotherapy Video Series and is intended solely for educational purposes for mental health professionals. In the video Dr. Bender employs a family-management approach to treat young clients with asthma.

Cancer
Pediatric Oncology Resource Center
Web site: http://www.acor.org/ped-onc
This is a website designed by parents of children with cancer that provides resources and information for parents, friends, and families of children who have or had childhood cancer. There are links for family support, information on childhood cancers, treatment issues, survivorship issues, and grief.

The National Children's Cancer Society
1015 Locust, Suite 600
St. Louis, MO 63101
Tel.: +1 314-241-1600
Fax: +1 314-241-1996
E-mail: krudd@children-cancer.org
Website: http://nationalchildrenscancersociety.com
This website provides educational publications, a message board, and frequently asked questions. In addition, the society promotes children's health through financial and in-kind assistance, advocacy, support services, and education.

Cystic Fibrosis

The Cystic Fibrosis Foundation
6931 Arlington Road
Bethesda, Maryland 20814
Tel.: +1 301-951-4422 or 800-FIGHT CF (800-344-4823)
Fax: +1 301-951-6378
E-mail: info@cff.org
Web site: www.cff.org
This website offers a section on publications and a video library which can help educate parents and children about cystic fibrosis.

Cysticfibrosis.com
E-mail: info@cysticfibrosis.com
Web site: www.cysticfibrosis.com
This website offers many educational and support options for children including forums, blogs, frequently asked questions, library, storyboard, art gallery, photo gallery, and a map to help locate the local CF center or chapter.

Diabetes

Children with Diabetes
Web site: www.childrenwithdiabetes.com
This website is an online community for kids, families, and adults with diabetes. Included on the website are chat rooms, forums, and care suggestions. The site also provides an option to explore the family support network and ask questions through the diabetes team.

Delamater, A. M. *Helping children manage diabetes*. Washington, DC: American Psychological Association.
APA Service Center
750 First Street, NE
Washington, DC 20002-4242
Tel.: +1 202-336-5510 or 800-374-2721
TDD/TTY: 202-336-6123
Fax: +1 202-336-5502
This video is part of the Behavioral Health and Health Counseling APA Psychotherapy Video Series and is intended solely for educational purposes for mental health professionals. In this video Dr. Delamater employs a developmental, social-cognitive approach with children and their parents to help children learn to live with and manage their own diabetes.

Sickle Cell Disease

Sickle Cell Disease Association of America, Inc.
Web site: http://www.sicklecelldisease.org
This website offers information about sickle cell disease, research articles about sickle cell disease, programs and services (including scholarship opportunities), links to medical sites and international agencies, and link to membership organizations located throughout the country. This site also contains a link to SickleCellKids. org which is a fun, educational, interactive website for children with sickle cell disease.

Advances in Psychotherapy – Evidence-Based Practice

Developed and edited in consultation with the Society of Clinical Psychology (APA Division 12).

Pricing / Standing Order Terms

Regular Prices: Single volume – US $ / € 24.95; Series Standing Order – US $ / € 19.95
APA D12 member prices: Single volume – $19.95; Series Standing Order – $17.95
With a Series Standing Order you will automatically be sent each new volume upon its release. After a minimum of 4 successive volumes, the Series Standing Order can be cancelled at any time. If you wish to pay by credit card, we will hold the details on file but your card will only be charged when a new volume actually ships.

Order Form (please check a box)

☐ I would like to place a Standing Order for the series at the special price of US $ / € 19.95 per volume, starting with volume no. ....

☐ I am a D12 Member and would like to place a Standing Order for the series at the special D12 Member Price of US $17.95 per volume, starting with volume no. ......
My APA membership no. is:

☐ I would like to order the following single volumes at the regular price of US $ / € 24.95 per volume.

☐ I am a D12 Member and would like to order the following single volumes at the special D12 Member Price of US $19.95 per volume.
My APA D12 membership no. is:

Qty.	Author / Title / ISBN	Price	Total
		Subtotal	
	WA residents add 8.8% sales tax		
	Shipping & handling:		
	USA — US $6.00 per volume (multiple copies: US $1.25 for each further copy)		
	Canada — US $8.00 per volume (multiple copies: US $2.00 for each further copy)		
	South America: — US $10.00 per volume (multiple copies: US $2.00 for each further copy)		
	Europe: — € 6.00 per volume (multiple copies: € 1.25 for each further copy)		
	Rest of the World: — € 8.00 per volume (multiple copies: € 1.50 for each further copy)		
		Total	

[ ] Check enclosed   [ ] Please bill me   Charge my: [ ] VISA   [ ] MC   [ ] AmEx

Card # _____ CVV2/CVC2/CID # _____ Exp date _____

Signature _____

Shipping address (please include phone & fax) _____

_____

_____

_____

_____

Order online at: **www.hhpub.com** or call toll-free **(800) 228-3749**
please quote "APT 2007" when ordering

HOGREFE

Hogrefe & Huber Publishers · 30 Amberwood Parkway · Ashland, OH 44805
Tel: (800) 228-3749 · Fax: (419) 281-6883
Hogrefe & Huber Publishers · Rohnsweg 25 · D-37085 Göttingen
Tel: +49 551 49 609-0 · Fax: +49 551 49 609-88
E-Mail: custserv@hogrefe.com